TOOLS FOR GODLY PARENTING

TOOLS FOR GODLY PARENTING

Erica C. Reynolds

DEDICATION

I dedicate this book to my family, who graciously allows me to grow in wisdom, as I parent.

- To my husband, Rev. Michael D. Reynolds, who is my partner in parenting our four children: Michael D. Reynolds II (wife, Alisa); Celenna Loggins (husband, Brandon); Jonathan Reynolds; and Cicely Reynolds. I also dedicate this book to our four beautiful grandchildren: Michael D. Reynolds III; Chloe Reynolds; Eric Loggins; and Levi Loggins.

I could not have written this book without our successful partnering experience in parenting. I appreciate the strong godly convictions and values you brought to the table. You are an answer to the prayers I prayed nightly as a child, asking God to bless me with a godly husband who loves the Lord and is committed to following godly principles. In you, God gave me exceedingly and abundantly above and beyond what I could ask or think in a husband. You were my groom for our journey together as godly parents and a committed couple. We were able to bring together our childhood experiences from godly families and dedicated parents. The parental reflections of both our parents created a map for successful parenting. But most important, you came to the table with your desire to be a hands-on Dad and a dedicated parenting partner. With this I was able to glean from your love of parenting, your love for family, your personal commitment, and your godly attributes. Thank you for your contribution to this wisdom I am able to share in this book. You will always be an inspiration and encouragement to what I strive to do. Your strength is a model of God's power working in us and through us, as we continue to parent. Your loving characteristics, your caring heart, your support, and dedication, helps to make our parenting enjoyable. It is an honor to now parent single adults and married adults, and to see them choose to reflect Christ in all they do.

• To Michael and Alisa Reynolds, who are doing a wonderful job of parenting, using godly principles. You diligently teach our grandchildren, Michael III and Chloe, to love the Lord, to obey, to believe in God's Word, and how to worship the Lord. Michael II, you reflect your dad's life in the godliest ways. I am so proud of how you lead your family with strength, dignity, and under the guidance of the Holy Spirit. You and my precious daughter-in-love, Alisa, have combined your godly childhood teachings to become a model of God's faithful promise.

• To Celenna and Brandon Loggins, who beautifully reflect great partnership, love, and commitment to God, as they enjoy their newest season of parenting. It is heartwarming to see your patience and hands-on approach to parenting our toddler grandson, Eric, and newest grandchild, baby Levi. You reflect godly parenting with meekness and dedication, as you continue to grow together in your parenting. Brandon, you are evidence of God's ability to answer our prayers of sending the ideal spouse for each of our children. It is rewarding to see you and Celenna reflect that passion for the things of God that was passed down through our family generations.

• To Jonathan Reynolds, my single adult son and minister of the gospel. It is a blessing to see you follow in your dad's footsteps of preaching and teaching in the ministry. You too have dedicated your entire life to working and serving in ministry with great compassion. You have sacrificed much for the Kingdom. I anticipate seeing what additional great things God will do with you in ministry. Watching you preach and teach the gospel helps to confirm how important it is for parents to faithfully teach the Word of God to their children.

- To my youngest daughter, Cicely Reynolds, who loves the Lord and whose life reflects God's loving heart for people. It is rewarding to see you as a gifted young artist, and a businesswoman. Your dad and I are proud of how you've set Christ as the head of your life. It is a blessing to receive the patience and care you give your parents. You have helped to make this book possible with motivation, as you checked on me daily, to see how my writing was coming along, listening and giving words of affirmation.

- Lastly, I dedicate this book to my aging mom, Magnolia Mosley. I have richly gleaned from the life of this once-Baptist-raised girl, who married into a Pentecostal family. She and my dad raised 11 children, in their God-fearing home. I am the oldest living daughter, the seventh child, and a student of the great teaching, training, and godly wisdom Mom provided me. My mom often called the entire family together, on our knees, for times of family prayer. We were also very involved in church, attending Sunday services, Bible study, youth group meetings, and other church events. Thank you, Mom, for the beautiful life you reflected, as a dedicated mother and godly woman. You and my dad, who died early in his life, were excellent models of godly parenting for me to reflect on while writing this book.

8

TABLE OF CONTENTS

Acknowledgments

I want to give thanks to the family and friends who have supported me during the writing of this book. Thank you for helping to stir up God's writing ability in me, to confirm it, to contribute, and to inspire me to launch into a new time of sharing some of the wisdom God has placed inside me over my years of parenting. I credit you for helping to make writing this book possible.

Thanks to Dr. Daniel Vassell and his wife, Jenny, author and singing artist, for inviting me to write this book for the Church of God's Mobilize Marriage and Family Conference. I am thankful for your inspiring me to write and to share the godly principles that have helped in our parenting journey. This work would not have been possible without the Church of God Division of Education and all those who worked actively to provide me with the support needed to pursue this goal. I am grateful to all those with whom I have had the pleasure to work during this book project.

Thanks to First Lady Lisa Adams, for the godly parenting wisdom she shared, for her pep talks, words of encouragement, and prayers, which have helped to give me confidence to complete this book project. Over the years, she has shared her inspiring parental experiences with me and others. Pastor Douglas and Lisa Adams have set an example of parental love, dedication, care, and sacrifice. Even when there were special needs, they continued to model God's endurance.

Thanks to Pastor Kimberly Short who has been a continual support, inspiration, and encouragement to Dr. Reynolds and me for writing projects. Your ongoing inspiration and support is always to be noted, affirmed, and appreciated.

Thanks to my daughter, Attorney Celenna Loggins, for her contribution to this book in allowing me to interview her and gain knowledge of newer parenting challenges of today, new generational perspectives, and innovative goals of this newest decade of parents.

—Erica C. Reynolds

INTRODUCTION

When we really look at parenting, we must agree there is much more to following God's Word to procreate ("be fruitful and multiply") than one might think. How are parents to do this today after their precious new baby is put into their arms, is strapped into its car seat, or settled in its nursery? This is a question I hope to answer with wisdom, in this book.

I was fresh out of college when we became new parents, beginning a new and unfamiliar chapter in our lives. My husband and I felt nervous and parentally naïve. When we were released to take our baby home from the hospital, we were pleased that the medical staff equipped us with sufficient instructions and supplies to begin the care of our newborn son. However, when he was only eight months old, I learned that I was pregnant again. At that time, my husband and I felt a desperate need for parental instructional tools. Thankfully, we were both raised in godly homes and were able to refer to a book that we were blessed to inherit. It is the best book to possess regarding parental instruction—the Bible.

The Bible gives us unswerving instructions on parenting; it talks about the godly ways to help make the journey easier. It has a wealth of knowledge about parenting God's way and how to raise our children. It teaches us how to train our children in the right way. Everything we need to know—from which teachings and values to teach our children to how to go about preparing them and raising them to be men and women of God, and how the Holy Spirit will guide parents to make the right decisions—is all found in the Word of God.

Good parenting is guiding our children into truth and righteousness. We've heard about many situations where a child has taken a wrong path. Still, because they had godly principles implanted in their hearts, they could find their way back to the right direction. It is in Proverbs 22:6, the Bible tells us: "Train up a child in the way he should go, and when he is old, he will not depart from it" (NKJV).

The Bible teaches us the significance of teaching our children about what is most important in this life. It is essential that we live a life that is pleasing to God. Colossians 1:10 says, "That ye might walk worthy of the Lord unto all pleasing, being fruitful in every good work, and increasing in the knowledge of God" (KJVS).

As parents, we can get stressed and overwhelmed, not realizing that God has already given us the answers for every parenting situation through the Bible. We have a tendency to look for solutions on parenting everywhere but in the Scriptures.

My husband and I have been parenting for more than four decades. We are now parents of adult children and grandchildren. I will admit that I have attempted some parenting fads, fashions, and even adopted some worldviews—many of which have faded away or changed. But, the ways of the Lord still stand to be accurate, and godly principles in the Word of God remain the same: "For I am the Lord, I change not" (Malachi 3:6 KJVS). God's Word never changes.

God's principles for parenting will stand the test of time and beyond. God's Word can be trusted to be the most significant resource among all parenting resources: "As for God, his way is perfect: the word of the Lord is tried: he is a buckler to all those that trust in him" (Psalm 18:30 KJVS).

Some of the godly principles needed for good parenting are commitment, personal relationships, godly teaching, reflecting Christ, sacrifice, love, and endurance. These will be fully addressed in the course of the book.

1

PARENTAL PERSPECTIVES

In reality, parenting is not an easy feat, and it's not for people who are not ready or willing. When it comes to godly parenting, it can be even more tasking and challenging. However, as believers, parenting is "easier" because we have Christ and help from above. In the course of the book, we will examine various tools that will enhance good parenting and ensure we raise godly children who will stick to the path of Christ and become activists for the Kingdom—children who will recognize, activate, and fulfill the purpose, and bring joy to the kingdom of Christ.

You may be wondering, *Why exactly do I need this book?* My parenting style may not be smooth, but it's not pitiable. I can continue like this and still rear fine children. Well, I am here to tell you that you are accountable to God about how you parent your children. Biblical instructions must be followed by parents to ensure their children tread in the path of the Lord. And, a little help with parenting isn't a bad idea. This book is a guide on godly parenting that will help you in the course of your parenting journey.

Traits

Various **traits** give parents the opportunity to break off disastrous parenting tactics and, in their place, create new and healthy tactics of parenting. Sometimes as parents, you find yourselves in situations where there are specific issues that arise with your children, and you wonder how exactly that particular incident happened. Various avoidable incidents with your children happen, not because of the present, but because of certain things that should have been done in times past—way earlier than the present moment. The decision of your child might be a result of specific choices that you have made as parents early in your parenting journey. But, do not worry, there is no situation that God cannot fix, because what God cannot do, does not exist. Your children at a given point in time will have to make decisions on their own, but it is your responsibility as a parent to encourage them and help them build up their character so that in the nearest future, they will solidly face whatever life throws at them and come out triumphant at the end. As a Christian parent, inculcating certain traits and ideas into your children will help shape their future attitude, since it is easy for children to pick up bad habits as they grow. But, the profound teachings they have received will help counteract the bad habits. If children just rely on their rational understanding, there will be countless mistakes they will make that will shift them from God's path. That is why as a parent, you need to let them know they cannot just rely on their nature as humans to run the race called life. If you want to be a parent who wants to raise children who are godly and can withstand the challenges of life, then there are certain traits that you must possess, and the beautiful part of it all is that they are biblical. Some parents are strong in some aspects of parenting and weak in others; the combination of these traits will enable a balanced parenting lifestyle. To effectively parent your children, you need to exhibit the following:

*One important **trait** that you must possess is **love.*** First John 4:10 says, "In this is love, not that we loved God, but that He loved us and sent His Son to be the propitiation for our sins" (NKJV). According to John the apostle in the above verse, he says that as believers, we learn to love by merely examining the love that God has shown us. The love that God has toward mankind is not conditional, and it is such a love that God sacrificed Jesus Christ in our place. And because you are familiar with the love of God, then it is time you show love to people around you and even people far from you. The moment your children discover that you are a love being, then it makes it easy for them to emulate you.

The love of God helps you as a parent to eradicate selfishness toward your children and other people. God's love is evident in His commitment and the sacrifice that He has made for us. And one significant way children learn about God's love is through the responsibilities and sacrifices that you make as a parent for them and the various teachings and training that you give them, as well as the sacrifices you encourage them to make.

*Another **trait** is **respect**.* Philippians 2:3 says, "Do nothing out of selfish ambition or vain conceit. Rather, in humility value others better than yourselves" (NIV). The apostle Paul admonishes believers that their thinking should be like that of Christ, and do unto others as we would want them to do to us. As a parent, when you give respect to your children, it helps bring out the best in them. Respect is more than just admitting that your child has done something worth applauding; it is about respecting your children because it is expected of you as they are also God's creation, and He loves them immensely. As a parent, when you have the trait of respect, it makes it easy for you to treat others like they are important and not like they are inferior to you. One sure way you can hurt the feelings of your children is by treating them like they are not useful for anything; a constant encouragement for your children is for you to let them know they are worthy and you value and respect them deeply. Respect comes in different forms, and an example is the way you address your family and people around you. Let your language be respectful; avoid condemning and cruel words regardless to whom you are referring and what you are trying to get across. The way you speak to your immediate family and people outside really matters as it is a means for you to train your children to respect people anytime.

Do you want to parent your children in the way of the Lord? *Then you need to possess the **trait** of **gratitude**.* Philippians 1:3-5 says, "I thank my God upon every remembrance of you, always in every prayer of mine for you all making my prayer with joy, for your fellowship in the gospel from the first day until now" (KJV). The apostle Paul is always grateful for the efforts of the Philippians toward him. Being grateful shouldn't always be because someone somewhere has done something good for you, but rather because it is part of your lifestyle and habit, and you are thankful regardless of the situation at hand. Gratitude helps breed a healthy relationship, and it also helps your children and family, as a whole, become selfless and have a united front against the world. When you are intentional about being grateful for every little thing people do for you and what God does for you, it will make it easy for your children to relate to how good God is and the wondrous things He does. When you are grateful, then it will be easy for you to praise God despite how you are feeling at that moment.

If you want to parent your children effectively, *then you must be someone who can **adapt quickly*** and is not overly materialistic or letting the things of this world worry you too much. Philippians 4:11 says, "Not that I speak in respect of want: for I have learned, in whatsoever state I am, therewith to be content" (KJV). The apostle Paul talked about being content regardless of the situation in which you find yourself. Your happiness should not be based on your current situation, your financial status, or your career. Train your children to quickly adapt to any situation in which they find themselves without letting the burden weigh them down. When you do this, it helps your children to encounter peace that is more than the challenges and tribulation seen in this world. When there is the peace, it lessens the worries that can lead to losing one's faith and trust in God. Adapting quickly to difficult situations gives you and your family the opportunity to go through the hard times and the good times together, and it enhances a higher level of faith and understanding.

*Another **trait** worthy of note is **being intentional** about certain things.* This simply means speaking up and acting out our values without giving room for external influences. If, as a parent, you possess this trait, then it will aid stability and consistency in your parenting style while building up your family. It also works well with other characteristics. As a parent, when you are intentional, it enhances concentration and increases wisdom to parent in a biblical way. That is why Colossians 1:10 says, "So that you may walk worthy of the Lord, fully pleasing to him, bearing fruit in every good work, and growing in the knowledge of God" (HCSB). You need to be involved in the lives of your children and what influences their actions. Don't be docile and expect things to fall in place by themselves; take charge and make decisions that will help boost the spirituality of your children.

*As a Christian parent, you need to be **forgiving**.* Matthew 6:14-15 says, "For if you forgive men their trespasses, your heavenly Father will also forgive you; but if you forgive not men their trespasses, neither will your Father forgive your trespasses" (KJV). Despite the fact that we were sinners, Christ still forgave us and died for us, and His love didn't diminish because of our sins and unfaithfulness. If our God is a forgiving Father, how much more should you as a parent be forgiving. You need to readily exemplify forgiveness to your children, regardless of the fact it isn't easy for humans to forgive. But from the Word of God there is an instruction to forgive others just as God forgives your sins.

Possessing these exceptional traits as a parent is essential for godly parenting. These traits will help you make right decisions regarding your children. When the Lord enhances you with wisdom, it isn't only to identify the various mistakes you have committed, but also to effectively correct them and make amendments. Likewise, in parenting, you will parent your children in a way that they can readily recognize their mistakes, and, as a result of these, avoid decisions that are disastrous to their lives. When you live out these traits, it will be easy for your children to mirror them and act accordingly.

Boundaries

In the Scriptures, Proverbs 22:6 says, "Train up a child in the way he should go: when he is old, he will not depart from it" (KJV). As parents, you should set clear-cut boundaries for your children. Help your children by undergoing a teaching process for them on lifestyles. And the longer you do this, the easier it is for them to abide by those teachings and live a life pleasing to you and to God. Most children will not make it obvious, but boundaries are sorely needed and appreciated by them. As adults, there is an understanding that comes with the presence of rules and this is because God has provided the Scriptures which will act as a guide for our day-to-day living and activities. Godly parenting for believers is exciting as an example to follow. It is the way and procedures through which God parents us; you can adopt the same procedures in parenting your children. You should be clear about what your children can do and what they cannot do. There should be a clear-cut understanding of what their limit is, and which things will have certain consequences. Don't get this wrong; it's not about being overly strict and preventing your children from mixing up or having fun; it's about enlisting the help of the Holy Spirit to aid your decisions on the boundaries that need to be put in place for your children.

Prayer is key: It is important to note that when it comes to godly parenting, nothing should be done without prayer, and this is the key to getting positive results in your parenting. Many Christian parents are worried about the end result of their children; they are scared about how their children will turn out when they become adults. So, if you are feeling like that now or you have thoughts along that line, do not be alarmed; there are many other parents with the same opinions. Parenting means being trusted with the lives of other people, and this automatically places a certain level of responsibility on you as a Christian parent. In reality, this can be really challenging; but do not fear, because the God who has placed you in the position of a parent will empower you to do an excellent job of parenting. Therefore, do not worry, just pray! Prayer moves mountains and makes the impossible, possible. According to the Scriptures, in Philippians 4:6, it says, "Be anxious for nothing, but in everything by prayer and supplication with thanksgiving, let your requests be made known to God" (NKJV). This part of the Scriptures talks extensively about what Christian parents really need in their uncertain times. This scripture is about the worry that stems from godly parenting. When you are afraid and unsure of the future of your children, you need to go to God in prayers and be explicit with your worries and fears and watch peace flood your body and soul.

Love your child unconditionally: When it comes to loving your children, you should love them, not because of specific attributes or characteristics, but because who they are—your children! This mirrors the way God loved us even while we were sinners, He loved us and died for us. As believers, we do not need to prove ourselves to God, because God loves us regardless of the situation. God loves us unconditionally, and so as godly parents, you must love your children without limit. It is the nature of God to love both the believers and unbelievers, so you should also do the same. God's nature teaches parents to love their children without conditions and reasons. Even though you discipline them, you should also let them know that no matter the situation that arises, your love for them is constant and unchangeable, just like God's love for mankind.

Forever is the deal: Let it be known that since you already decided to have children, you automatically have signed the contract of responsibility and commitment forever. You can't say I want to be a parent, but not all the time. We do not love our children for certain hours every day, no more, no less; we love our children forever. When it comes to commitment, your children will depend on you for their needs until they are adults. Even after they are adults, your parenting continues even to the point of death. Understanding this will make parenting easier for you as your mind is already prepared to know that it is for the long haul.

Being parents comes with a sense of responsibility and accountability. Every child is quite different and has unique traits and characteristics. And these traits can either be an appalling version or a voracious one. It is your role as a parent to eradicate the negative traits and nurture the positive ones to fruition, and this is not something you can do on your own. You need God's help and guidance to make this happen. It's not the will of God for you to keep struggling with parenting your children. He is our ever-present help in times of trouble, so reaching out to God when you need help with your children is the right way to go. Raise up matters to God in prayer concerning your children, as prayer is an avenue to communicate with God. This is one of the means to get a sense of bearing and direction.

Another tip to be considered is modeling godly behavior. As believers, we should replicate what Christ has taught us when it comes to parenting. Children are very observant and successfully mimic your actions and attitudes, so it is crucial to thoroughly do or say what you know is right for your children to do or say. Also, Christian parents must ensure that they meet the standard of Christ which must be taught to their children. There are certain things that you must teach them and let them be familiar with. Since you have made the promise to raise them up in the path of the Lord, you need to fulfill this by encouraging them to attend church, Sunday school classes, and Bible studies.

These children given to you are not yours; they belong to the Lord; you are a guardian whose responsibility is to cater to them and raise them to love the Lord. In the Book of Mark, Jesus himself said to His disciples, "Let the little children come to Me" (10:14 NKJV). This shows us that Jesus knows the importance of children and how they will expand the Kingdom. So, as parents aiding the progress of Kingdom work is essential. This book is explicit and will touch on practical ways through which godly parenting can be carried out—the do's and don'ts and the necessary things to know as Christian parents.

2

COMMIT TO TRUTHS

Commitment to Following God's Word

If we want to know what God says about good parenting and how to parent God's way, we need to commit to using the Bible as our manual and major source for leading and guiding us to becoming the best parents we could ever be. We do our best parenting following His principles through the Word of God and under the guidance of His Holy Spirit with Jesus Christ as our example. Through Christ, we will be successful in parenting. The Word of God says:

- "This book of the law shall not depart out of thy mouth; but thou shalt meditate therein day and night, that thou mayest observe to do according to all that is written therein: for then thou shalt make thy way prosperous, and then thou shalt have good success" (Joshua 1:8 KJVS).

- "For this cause also thank we God without ceasing, because, when ye received the word of God which ye heard of us, ye received it not as the word of men, but as it is in truth, the word of God, which effectually works also in you that believe" (1 Thessalonians 2:13 KJVS).

Following God's Word ought to be intentional, and making use of it in your parenting lifestyle is essential. Below are various ideas to be gleaned from the Word of God by Christian parents. Psalm 127:3 says, "Children are a heritage from the Lord, the fruit of the womb is a reward" (NKJV). For each child, there is a plan already in place by God and for parents, it is a gratifying job to parent God's children.

The thing is, when it comes to parenting, just like it is in marriage, there is no concrete manual from the beginning to the end. Experiences and training are gathered on the job. For some parents, they have exemplary parenting models from either their own parents or adults around them, while other parents have had to make do with parenting models that are not godly or positive in nature. The truth is, no model can fully mirror God's plan for parenting your children; only God can give you a model from the beginning to the end to make use of what will make your children love and honor God.

When it comes to parenting, it can be compared to growing a garden. To develop a beautiful garden, you will need to make use of your gardening experience to tend, weed, water, and nurture your garden. When it is about raising your children, you need to love, care, discipline, give your time and attention to your children, and then just keep the process going.

When it comes to godly parenting, the Bible helps to germinate the seeds that have been sown. According to the Scriptures, as Christian parents, you need to let your children know about the various works God has done in their lives. Tell the story of Father Abraham and the blessings for him and future generations which believers are part of.

Teach the Word of God

If you pride yourself on being a godly parent, then you need to make sure your children are taught the Word of God daily.

The Bible is a manual that is used for our day-to-day living. As a living being, you have a body, soul, and spirit, and you cannot nourish some part and let the others suffer. As godly parents, you need to also raise your children's spirit with the Word of God, not just physically by feeding them, clothing them, and giving them their essential needs. Don't leave the spiritual life of your child to chance or wait until they are old enough to decide for themselves. Whatever habit your child is used to will grow and expand, but introducing a foreign or new idea to your child when adulthood is already near is next to impossible. That is why the Bible says to train up your child in the way he should go so that when he grows, he won't depart from it. God expects you as a parent to be in charge of the spiritual welfare of your children, He expects you to train them, build them up in the ways of the Lord, and watch them develop and also help them up when they stumble on the way. It is more than just giving your children an education and taking them on vacations. Don't get it wrong, I am not saying going on holidays is not godly, far from it. I am saying for no reason should you ignore the spiritual growth of your children only to empower their physical existence ALONE! Balance the physical and the spiritual without being biased, and watch your children grow into the happiness of the Kingdom.

It is God's wish for believers to meditate on His Word, indoctrinate the children in the Word, discuss the Word with them, and incorporate it into their everyday lifestyle.

Deuteronomy 11:18-19 says,

> Therefore you shall lay up these words of mine in your heart and in your soul, and you shall bind them as a sign on your hand, and they shall be as frontlets between your eyes. You shall teach them to your children, speaking of them when you sit in your house, when you walk by the way, when you lie down, and when you rise up (NKJV).

This part talks about how it is scriptural to teach your children the Word of God whenever and wherever. By studying the Word of God, we know what God frowns at and what pleases Him. Learning more about the Scriptures also helps us know how to retrace our steps back to God when there is a need for it.

Give Direction

Another important thing that godly parents receive from studying the Word is how to lovingly direct the children.

Adults and children alike do not appreciate being constantly ridiculed, insulted, criticized, and demeaned. It is not the duty of parents to frequently discourage or incite their children. This might move the children to become negligent and refuse to even try to better their own lives since they believe that they will be criticized and ridiculed anyway. If you need to discipline your children, you need to carry this out in a godly manner. Regardless if your own parents were godly or ungodly, you as a parent must not replicate the characteristics and attributes of an ungodly parent; start a new, better trend that will give you the end result that you seek for your children.

If as a parent, you show love to your children when necessary, then it is expected of them to be obedient. Your love will help them build up their character in a positive way so they can honor God and man.

Be attentive to your child. You will regularly need to spend quality time with your children as this will make it easier for you to get through to your children without forcing them to listen. Do not think that a meager 20 minutes every week is enough for you to train up your children in the way of the Lord. You need to set aside time for devotions, fellowships, studying, and just enjoying each other's company for this to happen. To impart godly principles into the lives of your children, this will occur through your actions and the words you speak to them. If your actions do not correlate, it will be noticed by your children, and this can cause havoc at the end of the day.

To start with, you can discuss the following Bible verses with your children:

> Children obey your parents in the Lord, for this is right. Honor your Father and mother; which is the first commandment with promise; that it may be well with you and that you may live long on the earth. And you, fathers, do not provoke your children to wrath, but bring them up in the training and admonition of the Lord (Ephesians 6:1-4 NKJV).

If, as godly parents, you adhere to the instructions in the above passage, then parenting your children will be less challenging.

Comfort

Another duty of a godly parent, according to the Word of God, is to comfort His children. It isn't surprising that the Holy Spirit is referred to as the Comforter, as is exemplified in Isaiah 66:13, which says: "As one whom his mother comforts, so I will comfort you; and you shall be comforted in Jerusalem" (NKJV). The Holy Spirit promises to comfort everyone just as a mother comforts her child. This shows us that it is biblical and physically proper for a parent to soothe his/her child.

The world itself is full of ups and downs, and children need someone they can talk to, rely on, and most times, a shoulder to cry on. Children ought to know how to deal with challenges and difficulties while at home. This is a steppingstone that gives them the expertise needed to deal with and sort out challenges of the outside world.

Although you as a parent need to be the primary teacher in your child's life, there are many other people teaching in various capacities too. You have his schoolteachers, church members, and even people in your neighborhood. Some of those secondary teachers either reinforce your teachings or condemn them. In all these, a child might be unsure about what to really believe and follow, and that is the reason why I am urging you to lead your child by example as basically, children tend to be observant and imitate what they see. If your actions and your speech match, it will be easier for your child to know if and when an outside influence differs from the one regularly encountered in the home. Telling your child not to do something because it is terrible, and then you do the same thing is hypocritical. It should not be indulged in. If you do so, it will reduce the trust that your child has in you and might lead to disobedience in the near future. Let your child know that as you are ensuring that they know God, you also are trying to know God more.

Knowing that there are different personalities and temperaments should be considered when dealing with your children. Identify and understand your child's temperament, and instead of outrightly changing it, all you need to do is accept your child for who he is. Help him build his character. When it is common knowledge that you respect your child, comforting him won't be an issue.

When a child is aware that he is loved and accepted, it will be easy for him to condone the imperative discipline meted out to help him so he can become a better person. When you praise or reward your child for good behavior, it will lessen the need for discipline. For every good act carried out by your child, a word of affirmation or encouragement will go a long way in helping him to keep doing the good act. Praise him for being tidy, praise him for being truthful, and even praise him for looking out for his siblings.

Be careful not to say negative things to your children all the time, as it could make them feel like they aren't up to the standard you expect from them. There are examples of people who felt like the standard their parents raised for them was too high. It has unconsciously caused a strain in their relationship with their parents. To avoid a strain in the relationship with your children, you need to be conscious not to say any negative comments about them, continually belittle them, or compare them to their peers. You do not need to deceive your children and exaggerate things even if they are not doing well, but for each of their efforts and achievements, please remember to compliment them.

Provision

The next duty of a godly parent, according to the Word of God, is provision. As parents, you need to provide for your children and give them their needs according to your capability.

According to the scriptures in 1 Timothy 5:8, it says, "If anyone does not provide for his own, and especially for those of his household, he has denied the faith and is worse than an unbeliever" (NKJV). Meaning, it is imperative for parents to try to provide for their children as those children are placed in their hands to take care of until they can stand on their own feet, as well as take care of themselves. And for parents who refuse to provide for their children, it means they have denied the faith and are worse than unbelievers.

Be in Charge

Another duty for you as a godly parent is to be in charge of everything about your children. As seen in 1 Timothy 3:4-5, which says, "He must manage his own household well, keeping his children submissive and respectful in every way—for if [a man] does not know how to manage his own household, how can he take care of God's church?"(NRSV). Every godly parent should cultivate the habit of being in charge when it comes to their children, as they need to be an excellent example for their children.

Be assertive, do not be passive to the point where your child is unsure of what your stance is on specific issues about life and godliness. Joshua 24:15 says, "Now if you be unwilling to serve the Lord, choose this day whom you will serve, whether the gods your ancestors served in the region beyond the River or the gods of the Amorites in whose land you are living; but as for me and my household, we will serve the Lord" (NRSV). Joshua took charge of his family and made it known to all that he would serve the Lord with his family.

Putting God as the foundation of your family will make it healthy, and in turn, you will educate your children that God is in charge of their lives, and they should not go on engaging in activities that will not please God. Naturally, children want their parents to be in control. When this happens, they feel secure and have comfort in the fact that as a parent, you are willing to protect and coordinate their lives.

Also, from the Scriptures, it is known that as a godly parent, you should be able to correct your child. Proverbs 29:17 says: "Discipline your children, and they will give you rest; they will give delight to your heart" (NRSV). When we talk about discipline, we are not talking about punishment in its entirety as it has to do with giving rules, guidelines, and being firm when exercising those rules. Children need to be aware of what is expected of them.

When it comes to discipline, it needs to be taught very early for its effectiveness. There should be mutual agreement about discipline by parents. Just like God disciplines His children when they err, it is necessary to discipline your children to correct their paths and lead them in the ways of the Lord.

Commit to Godly Parenting

Regardless of how we are blessed to become parents—by procreation, adoption, marriage, guardianship, or spiritual parenting—godly parenting requires a commitment to use godly principles as the right tools for building, repairing, and maintaining a life of good parenting.

I enjoy watching DYI shows, and I have even attempted a few small projects myself. Something I have come to acknowledge is that useful tools are essential for any job. My husband comes from a family of carpenters. He makes sure our home is equipped with the best appropriate tools for any household repair job that may arise. I always love to see his face light up when it is time for him to go to the hardware store to refresh tools. Parenting is also Kingdom work, and parents can find joy in being refreshed daily using the godly tools of parenting found in the Word of God that was written under the inspiration of the Holy Spirit. The Bible tells us in (Romans 14:17 KJVS), "For the kingdom of God is not meat and drink, but righteousness, and peace, and joy in the Holy Ghost."

Godly parenting is engaging your children in a way that most accurately reflects the life and words of Jesus Christ. To parent in a way that pleases God, you must seek, depend on, and pursue Christ. By living like Jesus in front of your kids, you model godliness; by training them, you build godly character; and by loving them, you show Christ's compassion.

Just as a manager or steward does not own what they are managing, we do not own our children. The children belong to God, and we are entrusted with their care for some time. And we will be held accountable for the care we give them.

Much can be said about parenting; this may be based on culture, religion, worldviews, and even politics or laws.

With all the unprecedented immorality, anti-family, anti-parenting concepts in our schools, and the mixed parental views portrayed in our media, today's parenting can be challenging.

Technology also has modified the way we parent. It has become a force for good and evil. On the one hand, technology gives us access to the most extensive library in the world. On the other hand, through technology, we have unprecedented access to absolute evil. However, technology alone is not the culprit. It is the individual who uses technology which allows it to be able to communicate evil.

Today, we are a technological world. The world and our daily lives have been revolutionized by new developments in technology. Amazing tools and resources have put useful information at our fingertips. Computers are more higher-powered and even more portable. They have become increasingly faster. Smartphone and social media are commonly used by families.

More so, technology has made our lives easier, faster, better, and more fun. We depend on the Internet for our jobs, education, shopping, worship, and more. We have faced a world disease pandemic, and more people are now working from home. In this situation, the Internet and social media tools have become a means for our survival.

However, parents face new challenges and concerns as technology continues to emerge into our lives. Children between the ages of 6 and 23 fall into a generation now being labeled postmillennial or Generation Z or iGeneration. Parents face many challenges in shepherding these teens in the digital age.

The children born after the Internet was commercialized in 1995 have no pre-Internet memories. These children entered (or will enter) adolescence in the age of the smartphone and are more likely to be more digitally connected to a smartphone-addicted generation. How do we parent in a digital age? With God's help, how do we face the data-trends?

The danger we encounter today is a result of the marriage between technology and corrupt culture. Even though the tactics of the devil are bringing evil to everything possible, we can be assured that God is indeed in control. As Paul said: "All things will work together for good to those who love God and who are the called according to His purpose" (Romans 8:28 NKJV).

"But as for you, ye thought evil against me; but God meant it unto good, to bring to pass, as it is this day, to save much people alive" (Genesis 50:20 KJV). What the devil meant for evil, God can work it out for our good.

Ways to Ensure Godly Parenting in This Age of Technology
In the world where the iGeneration is taking over, as godly parents, you need to keep up with the trends to be able to curtail the excesses of your children when it comes to technology. The first thing you need to get done is to get the necessary education. I am not talking about classroom education here; I am referring to talking to your children and also learning a thing or two from them. When you listen to them talk, you will discover they fondly talk about the latest technology, how it is used and the way they prefer to use it. And as a parent who is concerned about the technological prowess of their children, you need to ask questions. There are various ways to get the answers you seek; there is a favorite saying that Google is your friend. Go online and research on multiple technologies, apps, sites, and devices your children make use of. Many parents are helpless when it comes to ensuring godly parenting in this age of technology, because they are ignorant of certain things and do not have the right knowledge to execute some roles as believers.

You need to be online on various social media platforms, get a Twitter, Facebook, WhatsApp, and other media that your child has and open an account. Follow their accounts, too, so this way, you can see the various contents they post online. Be interested in the multiple games your child plays online, so you can ascertain if it is violence oriented or not. Being educated about the world of technology will ensure that there isn't a wide gap between you and your child as mostly distance is due to ignorance on the part of the parent. So go online and try to interact with your child on various social media platforms.

Following your children online does not mean you have to have the same opinion about issues; it is just about being close by to correct them in case they are putting out content that is not godly. The whole idea of parenting is that you are close by when your children really need you. When it comes to your children and technology, you need to always try to react accordingly. It's not the use of technology that is bad, but the abuse of it by your child. Just because it is common knowledge that some people misuse some of these devices and technology, does not necessarily mean your child will also misuse those apps and sites. The moment you hear about those excesses and abuses, all you need do is have a discussion with your children and let them understand the disadvantages and consequences that are attached to the abuse of technology. Do not be overly aggressive; just use examples. Just as you would warn them of the dangers of driving, you too need to make sure they understand the dangers online or with various technologies. Another thing to do when it comes to parenting your children in this age of technology is not to be easily fooled or trusting. Overreaction could be a problem, but your child becoming dependent can be dangerous. The fact that your child is well-behaved and in a right place does not mean he or she cannot deviate from the path you have known them to travel. Your child can, at any point, go sideways with technology, and devices coupled with the type of friends they keep at any given point in time can cause problems. The ease and availability of technology can also invite the children to tread dark paths. Educating your children will help them know the vices and the consequences that abound, but really getting to know your children and keeping a close eye on how they make use of technology will prevent excessive use and abuse. If you are worried or have an inclination that your child is misusing the Internet, there are various websites and software that can help you keep track of their doings.

Ways of parenting in a godly manner in this jet age are challenging but doable. Try to know the friends that your children keep. Have you been in close contact with them and are you establishing a communication line with them? It is your responsibility to follow your children's friends on their social media handles too. This is not stalking; it is trying to identify the kind of influences they have on your children and if it is welcomed or to be rejected.

No one, I repeat, absolutely no one is an island of knowledge. Talk to other godly parents in the same category with you. You will be amazed at the number of things you can learn positively from them. Be inquisitive, talk about the challenges you are facing with your child and watch them tell you their experiences and how they have overcome it without too much stress. Listen to their answers and suggestions and make use of it in your parenting where it matters and is needed.

This might be a little sketchy, but I will advise that for children until their teenage years should be monitored online; you can start with having the passwords to their handles as this alone is enough to let them know they are under scrutiny and should act accordingly. When a child is stiffly against giving out their password to you as a parent, it is probably an indication that something is not right somewhere. Having their password doesn't necessarily mean you want to go through their chats and emails, but it is so you could if you wanted to. The more responsible your child becomes, the easier it is to let him or her have freedom. It is important to note that as a parent, it isn't every one of their pictures you need to comment on or like, as they need their share of fresh air too. Practically being involved in all their online life can be choking for them. So, just be the parent that understands everything; you don't necessarily have to be their best friends every day every time; give them time to catch up with friends and acquaintances too.

There is also practical day-by-day steps to curtail the excesses of the iGeneration when it comes to technology. One of those rules is to keep all devices out of the bedroom when it is bedtime. You can even set up the rule of 12 hours per day using tools like a 9:00 a.m. to 9:00 p.m. rule or something along that line. Help your children break their addiction to certain things like T.V, online games, movies, etc. Ensure they follow their sleeping routine and confiscate all gadgets when it's time to go to bed. There should be a set of rules that ought to be followed before using the mobile devices; expound on the behaviors expected of them as children of God and what they're expected to do with the tools they have with them.

The moment your children cannot find a sense of satisfaction in Christ, they will look for it somewhere else and in something else. Keep praying that the Holy Spirit will allow the love of God to be shed abroad in their hearts, so they will choose God above every distraction of the digital age. As a parent, you need to watch your own excessive use of devices before you can curb your child's excesses. Also, you need to make sure you remember to honor family traditions like vacations, dinners, and even rides. These outings and indoor activities should be a "no phones" moment. As a family, you get to have heart-to-heart discussions and talk about things ranging from school to getting to know each other better.

Below are other ways to ensure godly parenting in your home, aside from the physically related ones. As the Bible says in 2 Corinthians 10:4: "For the weapons of our warfare are not carnal but mighty in God for the pulling down strongholds, casting down arguments and every high thing that exalts itself against the knowledge of God, bringing every thought into captivity to the obedience of Christ" (NKJV).

Trusting in the Lord

- "Trust in the Lord with all thy heart, and lean not on your own understanding; in all your ways acknowledge Him, and He shall direct your paths" (Proverbs 3:5-6 NKJV).

- "As for God, his way is perfect; the word of the Lord is tried: he is a buckler to all them that trust in him" (2 Samuel 22:31 KJVS)

Know That the Lord Is Good

- "The Lord is good, a stronghold in the day of trouble; and He knows those who trust in Him" (Nahum 1:7 NKJV).

- "For the Lord is good; His mercy is everlasting, and His truth endures to all generations" (Psalm 100:5 NKJV).

No matter the challenge, the fall, or the fight, because of his mercy for us, I can trust that God will make it right. In the end, it will all be good.

Not Wavering

Many secular beliefs have come to be more recognized as a faith choice or inclusion to one's walk of faith.

Religious practice has dramatically declined in the United States in the last 50 years. However, spirituality appears to be more substantially faith-based than ever.

Today, one in three Americans under 35 years of age are religiously unaffiliated. These individuals do not identify with any formal religious group. A spiritual sentiment is healthy and growing. With the rise of computers, mobile apps, and the Internet, faith practices have gone increasingly high-tech. To access spiritual teachings and religious groups, we can use our mobile phones.

Pew Research found in a 2014 survey that some 20 percent of Americans shared their faith online in a given week. Sixty-one percent of millennials reported seeing others share their faith online. From Instagram accounts to podcasts to YouTube channels, there are more ways than ever to find and share spirituality.

Parents, when your children rebel or struggle, intentionally make a choice not to get engaged in the part of the adversary. Like the prodigal's father, ensure they know that you are for them, no matter what. One day when my 13-year old daughter told my husband and me that she no longer wanted to be a Christian, we were caught by surprise, because we thought we were doing a tremendous job parenting. What caused our daughter to feel that way in her heart? Where did those secular thoughts come from? As immature as the circumstance may have been, that helped us see our child's battle. She had begun to stay close to Jesus and now much pressure from the world was being applied to our godly child. The act gained my daughter a long one-on-one Bible study time with her dad, the pastor.

Today, our daughter is a successful attorney and a beautiful Christian mom of two, happily married to a godly man. It is rewarding to see the parent using divine principles.

It can be difficult, as Christian parents, to remain successfully committed to godly parenting, with the complications of raising children in a world of many faith beliefs, corruption, and battling the devil to stay close to Jesus.

The Bible is a favorite attack point of skeptics. Our children are hearing it said that the Bible is an ancient, irrelevant book filled with inaccuracies and contradictions. However, the writer of Hebrews tells us, "Be not carried about with divers and strange doctrines. For it is a good thing that the heart is established with grace; not with meats, which have not profited them that have been occupied therein" (13:9 KJVS).

Parents who genuinely commit to following godly principles will be successful. Successful parenting is godly parenting.

- "[God will] make you perfect in every good work to do his will, working in you that which is well-pleasing in his sight, through Jesus Christ; to whom be glory for ever and ever. Amen. (Hebrews 13:21 KJVS).

- "His way is perfect; the word of the Lord is tried: he is a buckler to all them that trust in him" (2 Samuel 22:31 KJVS).

The world around us may constantly be changing, but God is still the same today, yesterday, and forever.

- "Jesus Christ the same yesterday, and today, and forever" (Hebrews 13:8 KJVS).

God is our Master craftsman, maker, and creator, and He has laid-out for us the best tool for our task of parenting.

- "In the beginning was the Word, and the Word was with God, and the Word was God" (John 1:1 KJVS).

Parents, we can find our strength and ability in God's Word that says, "I can do all things through Christ who strengthens me" (Philippians 4:13 NKJV).

God will give you the ability to do good work.

3

A Personal Relationship

Godly parenting requires having a personal relationship with God. As we reflect God in our parenting, we will learn to be fulfilled by enjoying the incredible call of parenting, much like our heavenly Father.

Make your personal walk with God your priority. Godly parenting requires far more than tips and techniques; it begins with knowing Christ as your personal Savior. We are wrong to think that we can raise our children to become godly men and women without having a passion for Christ, a commitment to walk in righteousness, and a strong desire to obey His Word ourselves. His words must be in our hearts that we might not sin against God and that we may be able to be the best teacher to tell our children the truth.

There cannot be godly parenting unless you, as a parent, have a solid personal relationship with the Lord. As it is, what you have and what you have encountered is what you will share with your children. Without a personal relationship with Christ, it is evident you are just adhering to rules that have been rationally proven to ensure successful parenting, which in reality does not work for everyone and might lead to failure in your parenting abilities. To ensure a Christian home where godly parenting abounds, you should be sure the activities and dealings in your family reflect God's way. Some parents will encourage their children to do what they say, not what they do. This ideology is ultimately against the ideal purpose of God for the children entrusted into your hands. Check within yourself and decide if your plans fit into God's plan for your home. If not, then you need to retrace your steps before going ahead to tutor and mentor those children.

If you want to lead your child in your footsteps, then the first thing is to ensure you are on the right track too. When it comes to studying God's Word and you want your child to be a student of the Scriptures, then it means you too must be a student of the Scriptures. It means your children have seen you studying the Bible, so asking them to do the same will not be strange and new. You can even read together with them and share insight into what you have read.

Parents should walk the same path they have planned for their children, so it will be less challenging asking them to follow. Godly parenting has to do with meticulously following the rules that you have planned for your children. If there is a problem from the top, it will indeed affect those on the lower part of the link.

Praying Parents

Prayer is essential. It is compelling and extremely important. We do not want our children to be consumed by this world but instead have a deep relationship with Christ.

Romans 12:2 says, "Be not conformed to this world: but be ye transformed by the renewing of your mind, that ye may prove what is that good, and acceptable, and perfect, will of God" (KJVS).

Our children need prayer for resisting temptation, to make good friendships, to make right decisions, to stand firm in their faith, and to deal with the opposite sex. Parents should fight each battle through prayer. Pray with them. Pray over them. Pray often. Have them pray with you if they are willing. Prayer is the single most powerful spiritual weapon at your disposal. And the Bible tells us that the "weapons of our warfare are not carnal, but mighty through God to the pulling down of strong holds" (2 Corinthians 10:4 KJVS).

It is never too late to pray. Prayer is that open communication with God. Parents need to pray always. In 1 Thessalonians 5:17, the Bible tells us to "Pray without ceasing" (KJVS).

Parents should teach their children how to pray. Prayer is probably the most powerful tool they can use in their children's lives. They deal with the same temptations their parents do, and sometimes much more. God can guide them better than we ever could. The best gift we could ever give them is Jesus and pointing them to Him, because He alone will be their source of joy and peace when the world seems to be too overwhelming.

Psalm 5:3 says, "My voice shalt thou hear in the morning, O Lord; in the morning will I direct my prayer unto thee, and will look up" (KJVS).

Parents are often criticized for imposing their own values and religious practices upon their children. However, as Christians, we understand this to be a wicked tactic of the devil to discourage Christian parents from implanting God's truth and principles into the lives of their children. We are to teach our children that prayer does change things. In fact, the Word of God in Colossians 4:2 tells us to "Continue in prayer, and watch in the same with thanksgiving" (KJVS).

James says, "Confess your faults one to another, and pray one for another, that ye may be healed. The effectual fervent prayer of a righteous man avails much" (5:16 KJVS). Prayer is the most important thing to keep the family together; parents should raise their children to pray. Ask God for the wisdom needed to train up your child in a Christian manner, and also ask God to grant your child the heart to follow and grow.

Seek the Lord's help in raising your child, and you will have an alliance with the Lord. The moment you take charge of your own Christianity and build yourself up in your most holy faith, then it will be easier for you to help your children attain theirs. Make it a point of duty to let your child know that for every facet of life, prayer is needed. The truth is, you cannot be with your child 24/7, and you cannot be there to help them overcome challenges every single time! You cannot prevent what they are exposed to that can influence them when they are not close by.

So, all you can do is to pray for them and encourage them to pray for themselves. And in a world where there are troubles, challenges and tribulations, the best thing to do is pray until you get the desired result you seek. Communicate with God in your own way and watch him take control.

Study God's Word

We could judge our commitment by discerning how much time we spend keeping God's Word fresh on our hearts and minds. And, the time we do spend in His Word should be because we desire His Word instead of it being an obligation. Paul told Timothy, "Study to shew thyself approved unto God, a workman that needeth not to be ashamed, rightly dividing the word of truth (2 Timothy 2:15 KJVS).

Study to equip yourself as parents. Allow God through His Holy Spirit to direct you to find the biblical wisdom you need. I suggest you join Bible study groups, take advantage of online studies, and read adequate parenting resources, such as this one. Paul wrote, "My God shall supply all your need according to his riches in glory by Christ Jesus" (Philippians 4:19 KJVS).

It is a fact that when it comes to godly parenting, one of the most important things is to encourage a child to remain on the right path. The world is full of various influences contrary to Christianity, and the possibility of your child digressing is on the rise. Despite the training and the boundaries that you have put in place, you also need to study God's Word with your child and help grow his/her faith.

Do not let your child have the feeling they are isolated and alone in their Christian journey. Carve out time to have a heart-to-heart discussion about their faith, talk about the challenges you have faced in times past, and encourage them to share their own challenges with you. Be nonjudgmental and offer solutions that will make it worth their time. And the moment you see them backsliding, motivate and encourage them to go back to their Savior and Maker.

Feed your child with the Word of God and make use of examples from the Bible to answer their day-to-day questions.

Also, make use of your life experiences to exemplify things for your child. Children appreciate stories from the Bible and, most important, your own life stories.

It is essential that you as a family have a scripturally sound church to attend. The church will help emphasize all the biblical teaching you have given to your child. We have already established that godly parenting is a duty, but entirely possible with the right walk with the Lord and being a student of the Scriptures.

Christ-Centered Parenting

The writer of Proverbs says, "In the fear of the Lord is strong confidence: and his children shall have a place of refuge" (14:26 KJVS).

One of the benefits of raising a godly family is to make Christ their model. You can show them that you, too, need to rely on His perfection. "If we teach our children that Christ is the model, rather than ourselves, it takes the pressure off us to be perfect parents."

We may not always know exactly what's right for each of our children, but Jesus does. Living in a carnal society, it is easy to leave God out of the training of our children. Today's world challenges the application of God's laws whenever Jesus Christ is mentioned. History tells us that in 1962, the Supreme Court removed prayer from schools. In 1963, it removed the Bible; and in 1980, it removed the Ten Commandments from schools.

As parents, we do not have all the answers; we need God's wisdom daily to train our children in the way they should go. "For the Lord giveth wisdom: out of his mouth cometh knowledge and understanding" (Proverbs 2:6 KJVS).

It is quite genuinely impossible to be a "good" and "effective" parent without asking the Lord for His help and guidance in this secular world.

Christ-centered parenting needs to be carried out, but as parents, you wonder how to achieve this. Below are various ways or means through which you can wisely raise your children with Christ as a concrete foundation.

1. Do not just read the Bible in the hearing of your child, but also educate them on how to read the Bible themselves. And this begins with you. Do you know how to read the Bible and derive joy in doing it, or do you just read it so it will not be evident to people around you that you do not? Just like the recurring message in this book, you need to be a model for your children. Make sure they see you are reading the Bible often, and it will make it easier for you to encourage them to also go through the Word of God and learn from it. Show that you are passionate about the Scriptures, and then watch the passion spread to your children.

2. Families that pray together stay together; endeavor to pray with your children each and every day. It might not be straightforward initially, but after a little while you will see the unity and peace born out of family prayers and marvel. Many parents are prayer warriors, but they do it on their own without involving their children, thinking the children are too young or they can pray on their own, or they will slow the prayers down. From an early age, instill the habit of praying in unison with your children to encourage their faith in Christ. I am not saying you will not have personal prayers; no, all I am saying is there is a place of communal fellowship with the Father. And in years to come when you see your children join their hands and faith with others to agree over something, it will not be strange or new to you.

3. Do not shy away from specific talks that are beneficial to the spiritual growth of your children. Let them know about sin and its effects on the spiritual life of believers. Do not believe that what they do not know will not harm them. The most significant place for sin to thrive is in mediocrity; ignorance will help sin grow and breed as it is said that where there is no law and rule, then there is no sin. Most children will say God loves me unconditionally,

so it does not matter what I do wrong. Please educate your children on the consequences that are attached to sin. Let it be known that it was the sin Adam and Eve committed in the Garden that led to their separation from God, even though God still loved them after leaving the Garden. Make use of various biblical stories to drive home your point. Make sure your children know that sins are not to be kept secret; they are to be confessed. If sins are kept secret, the individual will not prosper. Teach the hardcore gospel, and let it be known that Jesus already shed His own blood for the remission of our sins. It would be heartbreaking if, as a saved person, they still go back into sin, it will defeat Jesus' sacrifice on the cross of Calvary. Sins should be despised; they are to be confessed and repented of.

4. Another thing that must be taught by parents in a Christ-centered setting is the love and compassion God has for mankind. God showed His love for mankind when He sent His only begotten Son to die in our stead (see John 3:16). Salvation cannot be attained by their good works, but they must accept Christ as their personal Savior and ask Him to dwell within them.

These teachings are in stages. You cannot bombard a 3-year old with what transpired between Pontius Pilate and Jesus. Teaching is in stages. For example, the very young, just need to know about the unconditional love of God. Teach them in songs and in recitals. For the more mature ones, let them understand the concept of God's love for them. John 3:16 is a useful reference for where to start. As they progress, you also equalize the teachings until they can grasp the whole ideology behind Christianity. In summary, teach your children to know what and who they are dealing with, let them be familiar with Jesus and His redemptive works.

5. There needs to be visible evidence of their salvation in their lives. You need to educate your children and let them know that true salvation bears lasting fruit, and that true believers are identified by the workings of the Holy Spirit within them. Teach your children in the way of the Lord and just trust the Lord with the result.

Obedience to God

Good parenting requires obeying the Word of God that commands us to train our children and obey the guidance of the Holy Spirit to lead us along the way. The Lord tells us in Psalm 32:8: "I will instruct thee and teach thee in the way which thou shalt go: I will guide thee with mine eye" (KJVS).

Obedience is better than sacrifice because losing our children to the world is a significant cost and loss. It can bring many unwanted consequences. But, God is good and He is holy. Godly parenting is doing things God's way to please Him. Therefore, we must find out what the Lord says in His Word, and we must obey Him by doing just what He says.

Moses taught the Israelites God's commands to help them live out godly lives among the heathen nations. Our standards must come from God's standards. As these commands have been taught to us, we need to teach them to our children.

Psalm 14:5 says, "There they are in great fear, for God is with the generation of the righteous" (NKJV).

John 14:21 says, "He who has My commandments and keeps them, it is he who loves Me. And he who loves Me will be loved by my Father, and I will love him and manifest Myself to him" (NKJV). Being obedient to God's Word has various advantages that cannot be ignored.

When we talk about being obedient to God and His Word, it merely means hearing the Word of God and adhering to it. It is about letting the will of God synchronize with yours and totally surrender to His authority and follow His will for us to train our children in the ways of the Lord.

 Obedience is an imperative attribute for believers, and it shows one's love for God. Often, obedience might see us sacrificing, disciplining, and moving out of our comfort zone to train and lead our children in the right path. Our decision to obey God concerning our children shows that we trust God even when it is tough and challenging. Another solid reason for obedience to God is because of the endless rewards that are attached to it. Whenever we obey the Lord due to our trust in Him, He ensures we are successful in whatever we begin. And even in the Scriptures, it is insightful to know that reading and obeying the Word of God will ensure that we are successful. That is why Jeremiah 29:11 says, "For I know the thoughts that I think toward you, says the Lord, thoughts of peace, and not of evil, to give you a future and a hope" (NKJV). His plan is to get us settled in every facet of our lives. God did not create you to fail in your parenting duties toward your children; He wants you to excel and succeed in that field to His glory. And for this to happen, there needs to be total obedience to His will and purpose for your life. Joshua 1:8 says, "This Book of the Law shall not depart from your mouth, but you shall meditate in it day and night, that you may observe to do according to all that is written in it. For then, you will make your way prosperous, and then you will have good success" (NKJV). This is God's promises for believers who obey him, and it is your responsibility to let your children know about the benefits and rewards that come with being obedient to the teachings of God.

Discipline

"Fathers, do not provoke your children to anger, but bring them up in the discipline and instruction of the Lord" (Ephesians 6:4 Amp.).

There are virtually going to be times when you get to be your child's friend, plus there are unavoidably going to be times when you have to be their disciplinarian. The balance between the two is that you learn to always be their God-given parent.

The second part of (Ephesians 6:4) says we are to raise our children in the "discipline" of the Lord, molding them into the likeness and holiness of Christ. In other words, we are to raise children in a way that helps them take their head knowledge and bring it into their lives.

I am personally a product of this principle. I was well-raised in a Christian home where we were active in church, taught at home how to worship God, pray, and seek God's face in the Word. Those values I continue to reflect in parenting my children.

Practicing good parenting that produces a "good" child comes from using God's truth. Your children will enjoy God's world, His gift of life, and learn to give many thanks to God.

We love our children so much that many times our love for them can cause us to let offenses go that should be disciplined. I found that my lack of energy after a long day can also affect how consistent I am with discipline.

The primary life lesson children will learn in discipline is that every action has a consequence: good or bad. This is how the real world works, but, it is best to show them and talk to them about these things in a godly way and let them learn what God says about whatever issues they are dealing with.

It is crucial that discipline always be connected with love, so our children understand we still love them, no matter what they do. However, there are still consequences for bad choices. This is how God disciplines us; likewise, we should discipline our children the same way.

All parents want the best for their children and want to raise them to have their best potential. The fantastic thing is that we have a God who does not leave us clueless to figure it out on our own when it comes to disciplining our children, but gives us a guide in the Bible. He loves our children more than we ever could, and we can trust Him to guide us in how to discipline them. We can train our children to show compassion and kindness, and we can train them to speak the truth in love and lead them to Jesus. He is the only one who can keep them from falling.

Discipline is a crucial part of parenting. When you ask people or you check the Internet, you will discover that various methods have been recommended to discipline your children to the extent where it can be a little overwhelming and difficult for a Christian home to pick the right choice for the family. And despite all you read online, including in this book, you still need to have your personal conviction birthed from the place of prayer and studying the Word of God. It is essential that you adhere to God's Word and follow His plan for raising a godly family and teaching the right principles to your children. The responsibility to train your child has been given to you by God, and by no means should you place the whole burden on their teachers from church. So, it is important for you to take charge and make sure you do not fail in your responsibility to God and your children.

When it comes to discipline according to the Word of God, you will need to start as early as possible. Do not wait until your child is a full-blown teenager before you think it is necessary to correct and discipline them. By that time, some habits will have been ingrained already, and to change them will be next to impossible since the child has been used to doing those things. When there is no rule of action or consequences and no fear of discipline from their training as a child, that child can begin to control and rule you since they feel they can do whatever they like regardless of the outcome. The way you respond to your child's needs and demands will determine if they will grow up selfish and being a manipulator or not. You do not need to wait for so long before instilling discipline into them. The moment they can readily know they have done something wrong, then you need to instill discipline.

Obedience by your child for your rules is essential, and they need to obey without grudging. Ephesians 6:1-2 says, "Children, obey your parents in the Lord: for this is right. Honor thy father and mother; (which is the first commandment with a promise)" (KJVS). Aside from your children obeying you, they need to do this with the right attitude, which is honor and obedience. This concept needs to be taught at a very tender age.

You, as a parent, should come to the understanding that children are different and do not react to things the same way. There is a uniqueness to each child, and it is left to you to discover your child's own personality. When a child is not familiar with the concept of discipline from home, it will be quite tedious to understand the idea and reality of salvation. As they will not see the need for salvation since they are doing right in their own eyes—all their actions are entirely okay. The response of a child to discipline varies; some are prompt, courteous, and remorseful, while some will want you to scream your lungs out before they decide to obey. So, if you have more than one child, you cannot expect them to react the same way to discipline and correction. Correct your child in a godly manner that you know is appropriate for the kind of personality he or she has. With time you will discover that a particular form of discipline works for one child but not the other. Positive reinforcement is one way to discipline your child in love.

This paragraph is crucial, and I will ask that you reread it just for emphasis. You need to be consistent in disciplining your children. Ephesians 6:4 says, "Fathers, do not provoke your children to anger, but bring them up in the discipline and instruction of the Lord" (Amp.). Have you thought about how you can provoke your children to anger unintentionally? This can happen when there is a certain level of ignorance. Be consistent about what you expect from them in terms of behavior. One day you do not find anything wrong with a particular behavior they have. Still, the next day, you are disciplining them for the same actions from the previous day. There is a sense of frustration that comes from not knowing what exactly is right and wrong. When you lack consistency in your discipline, it can provoke and infuriate your child and ultimately cause their anger. Refrain from it. Let them know if I do a certain thing, there is an inevitable consequence for it, and it doesn't change no matter the day or the time it is done or repeated.

You have been placed in charge of training your children, and you have authority over them. The wrong thing to do is to forget your self-control and start yelling at your children. It is already an established fact that you have authority over them, so all you need to do is take charge and make it happen. Yelling and screaming unnecessarily is like you are trying to prove to yourself that you are indeed in control.

Godly character is the first goal of the reasons why God created the family. God wanted us to learn more about Him in a group. The easiest way for children to really know about God is through their parents (immediate family), and this will take place from the start. The moment a child has a family that really unites under the canopy of salvation, then understanding the need for salvation will be easy.

The Bible says children are a heritage from the Lord (see Psalm 127:3). Jesus said in Matthew 19:14 to allow the little children to come to Him (NKJV). Therefore, parents have a serious duty to rear their children to know the Lord. May God bless you as you seek His will and way for your family.

4

GODLY TEACHING

Just as it is in Proverbs 20:11—"Even a child is known by his deeds, whether what he does is pure and right" (NKJV). A child's behavior is essential to God and should, therefore, be of great importance to parents. Our children's behavior is evident to onlookers. It is actually a part of our total testimony. As children begin to make sound moral judgments, they reflect the godly input you have been giving them even during their earlier years. Deuteronomy 6:6-7 says, "These commandments that I give you today are to be upon your hearts. Impress them on your children. Talk about them when you sit at home and when you walk along the road, when you lie down and when you get up" (NIV).

Teaching Worship

The home is the primary training environment. We should worship together with our children in our house—through music, singing, sharing the Word of God, and prayer. Around the table at mealtime is a good time to incorporate acts of family worship. Bedtimes are also good times to teach acts of worship as you read with them and pray with them. Travel times can be an excellent time for family worship. We occupied ourselves on our long road trips with worship songs, sharing favorite scriptures, listening to Bible stories, playing Bible trivia, and offering family prayer. Most important, we must teach our children how to live a life that worships God in all that we do.

The church plays a critical role in helping us in the accomplishment of our primary responsibility for Christian parenting. However, we must be part of a church that teaches participation in worshiping God.

We must expose our children continually to the presence of the Lord in corporate worship. They learn about God's kingdom work and experience the operation of the body of Christ. We made it a priority to allow our children to learn about living a life of worship through caring for others, sharing the gospel, giving to the church, and blessing others through giving. My children participated in feeding the hungry through the church's mission projects. They did walk-a-thons to help raise money for needy organizations; they help with giving out food baskets for the holidays, toy drive, and other mission-driven activities. As my children got older, we allowed them to raise their funds and go on out-of-the-country mission trips to help share the gospel. We should encourage our children to enjoy a life commitment to worship.

One of my most enjoyable worship memories as a child, was our weekly Friday night youth group gospel roller skating service. We skated to wonderful gospel and worship songs, the gospel Word preached, we had altar calls, and souls were won to the Lord. I was able to bring neighborhood kids along, several of whom live for Jesus Christ today. We should make sure worship is enjoyable and adaptable to reach our children. Help them to know worship as a blessing instead of a drudge.

We can teach our children to worship by teaching our children to love participating in church, to love worshiping at home, and to honor God by living a life of worship.

Engaging Kids in Worship

Most people believe that worship has to do with songs being sung in a solemn manner that is soul-warming and heart-touching. That is not entirely accurate since helping kids worship is beyond the songs and the rhythm. The purpose of the music used in worship for children is to teach God's Word and truth to kids. And it is also another avenue to know firsthand the efficacy of God's presence. And this is one of the reasons you ought to ensure that your children are fully active in the experience of worship. And worship sessions in churches should be experienced with zeal and enthusiasm as many people are not regular attendees and need to be trained and encouraged to follow Jesus despite all odds. This brings to the forefront the necessity of worship in ministry. As parents, you need to fully understand the practicality of worship sessions with your children and know how to interest them and engage them in worship.

It has already been established in the Scriptures that worship is not just music; it is a lifestyle. Worship has to do with the action itself, not where it occurred. Engaging your children in worship should not be tedious. If children, until they attain adulthood, understand music as being synonymous with worship, they will tend to relate with it much easier. When selecting the best song for your worship session with your children, it is better to have chosen the selection way before the time of worship; thus, it will eradicate the idea of worship being a chore or a task. And do not leave the choice of music to your child as they need you to be in charge and direct them, instead of giving them free rein to do as they like. Not having everything already figured out can harm the readiness of the children.

When it is the choice of songs, you need to consider the age range of your children and if they will understand the idea and wording. And for children whose understanding cannot comprehend certain music, then you should teach them about specific words and phrases beforehand. Just try to place yourself in their shoes to determine how to engage them in a worship session. Music ranges from the love of God to faith and peace and as they grow older, they understand the more matured ideologies of Christianity. Point out scriptural verses from where the inspiration of the words was taken, and precisely what it means, or the information it is trying to get across. Doing this will help your children understand, and the next time they come across the songs, it will be easy to relate to it. Make use of songs that encompass God's Word and talk about biblical truths.

Do well to repeat songs during worship sessions with your children; as I said earlier, when a child is familiar with a particular song, they will remember the teaching behind the song from previous times. Repetition is critical and it is mostly used for the purpose of emphasis. Another easy way to engage your children in worship sessions is to make use of motions. You may wonder how this helps with your children in worship. When children are making use of music for worship, and it includes specific movement and steps, it helps reinforce what the song is trying to say. And, the moment there is movement or rhyme with the wording of the music, it makes it easier for children to really personalize the meaning and act accordingly.

Children model what they see from their parents regularly. If you use the method of motion to instill worship in your children, then it means you need to do accordingly even though as an adult you do not really need motions to worship. If you disassociate yourself from these things during worship, the children will think it is okay to do so.

Sometimes motion worshiping is excellent, but there are other times children need to know that we worship by standing still and singing. Let your child know that both singing with motion and being still while praying are acceptable ways of worshiping, and it will help develop lifelong worshipers. Teaching the two styles is not bad, but as a parent, you are aware of what works for your children. So engage in worship sessions that you know will easily resonate with your child, ranging from the type of songs to the location, and to the method of worshiping. Be flexible to work with whatever works for your children.

Teaching at Home

Home is the ideal place for children to naturally learn to get along with others, learn work skills, social skills, manners, good attitudes, and much more.

Home is where parents model being a Christian and, in turn, present to their children the knowledge and practical opportunities to develop these truths in their own lives. Let your home be filled with Christian music. Sing to the Lord with your children. Teach them to worship. Teach them to pray at meals, at bedtimes, for needs ... relating the Lord to their everyday lives and activities. Spend devotional time with each child personally. Pray with them, read the Bible with them.

Parents should study the Bible with their children. Even if parents know Bible study is significant, statistics show that only one in every ten Christian families study the Bible together in a given week. If your children see you neglect to prioritize engagement of the Bible in your lives, they will have little reason to see it as the authoritative book Christians claim it to be. It is absolutely pointless to talk about the Bible being God's Word if you are not treating it as such. If you are not regularly studying the Bible with your children, there is a good chance they will eventually stop caring what it has to say.

Do not be afraid to get help from Bible training organizations. Some parents enroll their children with different ministry activities to help them grow in the knowledge of God's Word. I regularly involved my children in children's ministries, outside children and youth groups at church. I enrolled my children in Christian Bible-believing programs, such as neighborhood VBS, summer camps, Sunday schools, and Awana. These ministries were great for helping my children to memorize scriptures and to enjoy being nourished in the instruction of the Lord.

In Ephesians 6:4, Paul instructs parents to "bring them up in the training and instruction of the Lord" or other translations say, "nourish them in the instruction and admonition of the Lord." Any way you look at it, we are to teach them God's instructions! This means teaching the Bible to your child in age-appropriate forms.

Children would not learn the gospel without hearing it. Not only on Sundays but every day. Paul asks, in Romans 10:14, "How, then, can they call on the one they have not believed in? And how can they believe in the one of whom they have not heard? And how can they hear without someone preaching to them?" (NIV).

Regularly share the gospel with your children. When you are driving them to sports practice and tucking them into bed, take advantage of every captive moment with them to the teach about Christ.

Build up Godly Teaching in Your Home

Your homes have much to say about you, through your routines, arrangements, and activities that you carry out inside your home. They talk about your belief system. In fact, believers' homes should be witnesses to the world that the occupants are children of God and are actively serving God. Parenting should be about God, His will, purpose, and His Word. Your home should be a place where worship abounds instead of where you and your family wine and dine. What are some ways to build up godly teaching in your home?

It is commonplace to have several things vying for the top spot in our lives, ranging from convenience to wealth to entertainment and other things. They rival for position with God in your life, and sometimes they hinder you from respecting and giving God the honor He so deserves in your homes. Most parents prefer Netflix and Chill to having a moment of studying God's Word. Several other things take the place of teaching and training your children in the ways of the Lord. It is your responsibility to worship God without rivalry with other material things trying to take charge of your home and life. Focus on something that will endure for eternity rather than material things that cannot last a lifetime. Subscribe to reading and understanding the Scriptures, worshiping God in Spirit and in truth, and building up your most holy faith. So, for everything that tries to take up the position of God in your life and in your home, you must eradicate them or keep them under control. And most important, you need to teach the same thing to your children. There should be a level of self-control that will prevent movies, games, and other things from taking up the spot where God should be.

In 1 Corinthians 13, it says,

> Love is patient and kind. Love is not jealous or boastful or proud or rude. It does not demand its own way. It is not irritable, and it keeps no record

of being wronged. It does not rejoice about injustice but rejoices whenever the truth wins out. Love never gives up, never loses faith, is always hopeful, and endures through every circumstance" (NLT).

Another way to build up godly teaching in your home is to live your life, acting out the unconditional love of God toward other people. In your words and actions toward your children and other people, you need to portray Christ and His love. The passage above talks about how to practice this biblical love by being patient with your children, forgiving them of their offenses, and not holding it against them. We should always be hopeful and have the assurance of better days ahead for them. When you adhere to the instructions available in the Scriptures in parenting your children, you will quickly draw their hearts to Christ and have peace on all sides.

When it comes to parenting, what is being done regularly in the home will influence your child either positively or negatively. And whatever tradition you uphold in the house has a way of rubbing off on your children. In building up godly teaching in your home, you need to make the Bible the basis for your actions. Sometimes when you need help in carrying out your parenting duties, you run to the Internet to learn a trick or two to help you out. But have you for once sat down to think about what the Bible has said about things like that? For wherever you find yourself in the parenting cycle, the Bible always has a solution. You should make your children aware that the Bible is the standard every day and every time. For every tradition carried out in your home, every rule adhered to, and every ideology and belief should have its root in the Scriptures. Your stance on discipline and every other controversial thing should stem from the Scriptures.

It is your responsibility as a parent to let your children be aware that the truth is not from the ideas on the Internet or the opinion of friends and acquaintances. The truth is from the Word of God, and this will sink in faster if you refer your children to the Word of God for answers to their questions. This will send a message that the Bible contains the answer to all questions.

Building up godly teaching in your home and with your children is a challenge that must be accepted without reluctance. You need to see the world in light of the Scriptures. If, as a parent, you regularly fill your mind and that of your children with information that does not have its basis in the Bible and portrays an anti-biblical worldview, then a time will come when the children will want to conform to the things of the world. This is because their hearts are filled with things that do not have their bases in the Scriptures.

You are in charge of your homes and you have the power to prevent some things from having access to your home. You need to screen the content your children consume, as well as the type of friends they keep. It is your responsibility to protect your children from any attempts at corrupting their hearts and minds. You would do well to keep them occupied with books, programs, and music that will encourage them to fix their gaze on heavenly things.

Whatever you do for your children, you need to teach them the Word of God so they can be conversant with it and can obey the instructions therein. As parents, you need to teach the Law and Commandments of the Lord to your children either through everyday Bible studying or by other means. When there is enough time, feed your children with the Word of God, coupled with instances that will make it understandable.

When it comes to building up godly teaching in your home, then you need to fill your home up with worship and praises. Encourage your children to play an instrument if and when they have the desire for it. Worship is a powerful tool that ascertains our unwavering trust and faith in God. We are constantly reminded of our inheritance in Christ Jesus and encouraged to care for Him since He cared first. You need to put into remembrance God's Word and His promises that He has made to His people. Decorating your house with the Scriptures, will help you to remember them. It is also one way to beautify your home with them. Think about filling your child's room with snippets of the scriptures hanging and pasted in various corners. Its usefulness is that it acts as a reminder of who we are in Christ Jesus. I mean our position as sons and joint heirs to the kingdom.

How can your children be godly if you do not pray for them? Even the Scriptures say to pray for Israel, and it will prosper. There is a war raging for who controls the mind of your child, so there is the need for you to pray away negative influences since prayer is that tool that weakens and makes our enemies defenseless. That is why the Bible explains that the weapon of our warfare is not carnal. The moment you begin to pray the Word of God over your children, then it translates to the fact that you are praying God's promises over them. You are in charge of praying that the love of God is shed abroad in the heart of your children, that they will love the Lord and do great exploits in His name. You should also commit your children to the Lord to keep them safe and grow in wisdom and knowledge.

Practicing What We Teach

Parents or guardians love to talk about what is right and wrong. They can be quick to judge their children's actions, yet many times they do not look at themselves to see if they are modeling what they are teaching. Hence, the simple lessons that we instruct them about forgiveness, kindness, and how to react when they are angry or hurt tends to be the lessons we struggle with the most.

After our children are grown, parents are still present in their lives through the characteristics they reflected and instilled in their children while they were young, as well as through their ongoing relationship with their adult children. Have you ever stopped to say, "I said that the same way my mom says it"? It is often that I see a reflection of my mom or dad's facial expressions or body jesters in my face, the life I live, and things I do.

Our kids are consistently watching us to see how we tend to react in challenging situations, how we speak with our mouths, and how we treat others. We have to focus on practicing what we preach to be a "light" to our children as we train them to be a "light" in this world.

Do not be hypocritical

From the time when children are tiny, they have already started imitating others, as that is how they learn to behave, take care of themselves, and communicate with others. From the time your child is a baby, they observe you and other important people around them and tend to adjust their own behavior to the ones they have imitated from you and others. And it is essential to note that your actions and inactions go a long way in shaping your child's actions for a very long time. Since it has already been established that children tend to imitate things done by the important people in their lives, then it is your responsibility as a parent to ensure that there are amazing things your child can imitate from you.

As a parent, you need to be a person who, when your child is exactly like you, you will not have a problem with it. And because you are always under scrutiny by your child, then it is highly important that you live an exemplary life that is worthy of emulation by your children. Whatever good virtue you want to teach your children, then you need to possess it, and this is because you are the book your children are reading. If you want your children to be responsible, loving, and compassionate, then all those traits must be present in your own life. When they see it, then it is easier for them to imitate it, since it is not strange to them. What is the use of telling your children to be kind to their fellow human beings and treat them with respect when you, as their parent, are rude and uncultured? That is you being hypocritical and inconsistent, and it can have an adverse effect on the children. Practice what you preach and own up to your mistakes when you make them. Do not confuse those children with your unstable lifestyle, be true to your words and be a model worthy of emulation.

When you are inconsistent in your teachings and your actions, you are sending a signal to your children that it's okay to say one thing and do something else. This is not a right ideology for your child to possess, so you owe it to them to be consistent in your words and actions. Your attitude as a parent is the reference point for your child, as it is easier to remember your actions than your teachings. Your child needs to see you communicating with others positively and healthily while also showing care and affection so he or she can also learn how to be positive-minded and relate with people in love and unity. You need to be conscious of your words and actions because in the near future, your child might have patterned quite a number of his or her behaviors after your own.

Teaching by Example

Parents love to talk about what is right and wrong and can be quick to judge their children's actions. Still, many times they do not look at themselves to see if they are even modeling what they are teaching. The simple lessons that we teach them about forgiveness, kindness, and how to react when they are angry or hurt, tend to be the lessons we struggle with the most.

Our children are always watching us to see how we react in challenging situations, how we speak with our mouths, and how we treat others. We have to focus on practicing what we preach to be a "light" to our children as we train them to be a "light" in this world.

Your enthusiasm and love for Christ will make an impression on your children. When you are empathetic and respectful, it will rub off on your children as they watch you like that. When you are fond of insulting and cursing various people around you, it will not be a big deal for your son or daughter to do the same to people around them. Educate your children that it is better to communicate with another person if they have offended them instead of speaking ill behind their backs. Giving back to society is another way for you to teach your children by example, let them know that from the little you have financially and even spiritually you can make a difference in the world today. You can join missionary journeys and other nonprofit quests and let your child tag along to understand there is a sense of satisfaction that comes from giving back to society.

You can also teach your children by example, in the area of time management. Let your daily activities show your kids that life is more than just lazing around or being on the Internet for a long time. If you are in front of the T.V, more than half the day, how do you want to convince your children that they need to do other beneficial things with their life and time? Let them see you reading the Bible and other books, gardening, and even cleaning.

As a parent, you must be truthful and ALWAYS keep your word. The moment when you have promised something either to your child or someone else, you should try to bring the promise to fruition as your children will subtly pick up on this. If you want your child to be trustworthy, then you need to a trustworthy person yourself. And if for some reason you cannot keep any promise you have made to your child, then you need to sit down and explain why that has happened. This will give them the idea that they need to be accountable whenever they cannot meet up to a word that they have given. Be less materialistic, so your children do not think the sole source of happiness is from getting the latest gadgets and things generally. Be grateful for the little things of life.

5

REFLECTING CHRIST

Godly parenting is not merely a matter of external effort and method. Still, it involves reflecting our heavenly Father to our earthly children through our love, care, discipline, and godly training. Deuteronomy 6:6 says, "And these words which I am command you today shall be in your heart.

We could go through ups and downs in our spiritual lives, but the test is how much we really love God through the ups and downs. I made the conscious decision to ensure I show my children humility by allowing them to hear me say I am sorry when I am wrong. I regularly use the phrase, "I am miserable" with them in our relationship, and I encourage them to do the same. It is vital for children to witness their parents apologizing to each other. Children need to understand that it is natural to make mistakes or to even disagree sometimes. However, we should be humble enough to openly admit our wrong. Humility is a critical characteristic of living a life of obedience to the authorities and to God. "By humility and the fear of the Lord are riches, and honor, and life, (Proverbs 22:4 KJVS).

Training That Reflects Christ

Be certain your children know of God's excellent plan for their lives and understand your goal to help them grow in God's will.

The sooner you can establish a clear understanding between child and parent that the parent's role is to aid the child to accomplish God's plan for their lives, there can be a sense of unity and peace even during a storm. Proverbs 22:6 says, "Train up a child in the way he should go" (KJV). What is the way? Jesus answers in John 14:6: "I am the way, the truth, and the life. No one comes to the Father except through Me" (NKJV).

Good parenting is parenting with Jesus. He is literally called the Way in Scripture. There is no other way that pleases God.

Plant trust and confidence in your child's heart, so they understand you care about them and their future.

Looking at the second part of Ephesians 6:4, we are to raise our children in the "discipline" of the Lord, molding them into the likeness, as well as holiness, of Christ. In other words, we are to raise children in a way that aids them to take their head knowledge and bring it into their lives.

You might never see those seeds grow until the times of struggle come in their lives, but they will want to trust you rather than resent you.

It is important to tell your children often that God has something special planned for their future. Ask them about their dreams, desires, and ideas of what they think God might want to do with their lives. When parenting does not reflect Christ, it might lead to the children's rebellion.

6

SACRIFICE

Godly parenting is a life of many sacrifices for the natural and spiritual welfare of the children God has placed in your care. This great responsibility does not come without your giving of your time, money, heart, substance, and care. Sometimes in parent's sacrifice of some dreams or putting them on hold; they may need to reinvent themselves.

A heart of sacrifice is essential. Some parents have gone as far as to risk their lives for the sake of protecting or saving their child's life. On the other hand, some have not come to recognize the need for sacrifices in parenting soon enough.

The parent paying school tuition to have his/her child enrolled in a private Christian school is a sacrifice for many parents. However, for some children, being enrolled in a Christian school was their only means for learning godly principles. As a Christian school teacher, I have always had children in my classroom who did not come from Christian homes. Each year, I made it my mission to help implant the Word of God in each of my students' hearts and pray that not any of them would be lost.

Getting to know different families in my years of teaching has allowed me to meet parents who in their striving to climb the ladder of success, neglected some of their parental obligations. These involved making sacrifices in their schedules for their children in different problematic learning situations. Good parenting requires making sacrifices of our own dreams to give more attention to the needs of our children. Parents should not look to the educators and institutes to meet all of each child's needs.

It is a mistake to think that we could raise our children to become godly men and women without having a passion for God and His Word ourselves.

God's words must be on our hearts, for us to be able to implant it in the hearts of our children, and we must be willing to make the sacrifices.

It was my plan, after college, to have a career and to work a few years before having children, so I could climb a career ladder; I had planned to become a full-time career working mom, successfully balancing parenting and career, in the wisdom of God. However, when my children were young and only 17 months apart, I felt the need to make being home with my children my first priority. I sacrificed some of my own dreams and worked only part-time jobs, so I could meet the needs of my children. Later, when we became empty-nesters, I was at that time able to have a rewarding full-time teaching career.

Parents have to make decisions based on who they are, as well as their professions, character, the call of God on their lives, their gifts and talents, and the needs of their family to make the best decisions about sacrifices needed in their parenting journey.

Without any doubt, God holds parents responsible for guiding their children in the ways of the Lord. We must not forget our responsibility, according to Proverbs 22:6: "Train up a child in the way he should go: and when he is old, he will not depart from it" (KJVS).

In facing the Coronavirus pandemic, several states have required children to do online classes at home. Could this be so parents will be challenged and given a redirecting opportunity to personally focus more time and attention on their own children's training and educational needs?

We have become a dual parent/career world, leaving much of our child's training to others. I've taught for several years and have had discussions with parents who have made only a little time for their child's training.

However, we must look at the growing new challenges facing our parents over the last few decades. The world has changed, and society has made it more challenging to parent today. Our newer generation of parents have to decide the size of their family based on their ability to produce wealth. In our past decades, statistics have shown more impoverished families having larger families. Still, today, we see the rich and the famous having larger families and hiring nannies to help raise their children. Is the parent becoming less affordable for most families? One must ask, where are we going as a society regarding parenting?

We do not have as many government programs as before to help support lower-income families. More parents are needing to make their procreation decisions based on their finances. For many parents, having children can become a ticket to poverty. The cost of homes is unaffordable for the average single-income family, causing both parents to have to work full-time jobs. Several parents with post-college degrees are carrying large school loan debts and facing the high cost of childcare, not to consider mentioning private or Christian school. Who can afford to buy into the best school districts anymore? And, are charter schools no more than today's replacement name for the public schools.

Some lower-income families are in a situation where both parents work full-time and part-time jobs to try to live their American dream.

We live in a society that does not encourage both career and parenting.

I cannot help noticing an increase in baby showers and birthday parties to think that perhaps for lower than average to lower-income families, these parties are means for provision due to the high cost of diapers, baby care items, children's clothes, formula, and toys.

Yet, parenting necessitates being present with our children and providing for them, as well. The entire story of Scripture is entirely bound up with God's presence with us. He made us to live in it and enjoy it. Then, after the Fall, humankind was expelled from it. Via redemption in Christ, we are reconciled to God and restored to live in it.

Sometimes, we need to be prepared to make those unexpected sacrifices. For me, it came with deciding to homeschool again.

I had already homeschooled my first three children for a season while they were in grammar school. However, with already being in school to complete his Doctor of Ministry degree, my husband began planting a church. In this work, we were called to devote much time and attention to pastoring, so I began to feel overwhelmed. I was homeschooling three-grade-school children while parenting a toddler. Staying on track with school lessons became a juggle. It was then we made the decision to enroll our children in a Christian School. We were pleased with our decision to send them to a Christian school, but as our fourth child reached the third grade, we were given the news that our third-grader had problems focusing in the classroom. It was a moment to remember! I sat with her older-aged lady teacher, during the school's parent-teacher conference, and this woman took my hand, looked me in the eyes, and spoke with a quiet, still voice to me, advising me to homeschool my child. She shared how she had seen my daughter's type of case before and explained how some children in her situation do better in a one-on-one homeschooling environment. I took her out at the end of that semester, homeschooled her through much of her high school years. Today, she is a college graduate and a successful businesswoman. She is also an entrepreneur, building her creative arts and dance studio. I find it to be a joy being able to watch how the Lord has blessed the fruits of my labor. That sacrifice to homeschool again was great at that time in my life, because it meant my stepping back from some ministry responsibilities that I enjoyed doing, releasing some delicate ministry tasks to others, making financial sacrifices, and not being able to attend some social events. However, my commitment to do godly parenting was and is the top priority.

Parents need to make their own sacrifices based on who they are, their professions, character, call of God on their lives, their gifts and talents, and the needs of their family to make the best choices in the sacrifices needed in their parenting journey.

Without any doubt, God holds parents responsible for guiding their children in the ways of the Lord. We must not forget our responsibility, according to Proverbs 22:6: "Train up a child in the way he should go: and when he is old, he will not depart from it" (KJVS).

7

LOVE

Godly parents reflect the heavenly Father's love by telling their children they are deeply loved and delighted with them. God delights in us, and godly parenting means actual delight in our children. "Delight thyself also in the Lord; he shall give thee the desires of thine heart" (Psalm 37:4 KJVS).

A strong and pure heart provides stability in your family. "Keep thy heart with all diligence; for out of it are the issues of life" (Proverbs 4:23 KJVS).

That Christ may dwell in your hearts by faith; that ye, being rooted and grounded in love" (Ephesians 3:17 KJVS

Let the dominant tone of the relationship with your child be one of delight. Your children should not only feel instruction and correction, but they should also feel cherished, admired, and appreciated.

The Love of Christ

Jesus welcomed children with open arms and opposed His own culture to commend childlikeness. Matthew 19:14 says, "But Jesus said, suffer little children, and forbid them not, to come unto me: for of such is the kingdom of heaven" (KJVS).

> And Jesus called a little child unto him, and set him in the midst of them, and said, Verily I say unto you, except ye be converted, and become as little children, ye shall not enter into the kingdom of heaven. Whosoever, therefore, shall humble himself as this little child, the same is greatest in the kingdom of heaven (Matthew 18:2-4 KJVS).

We learn to parent God's way by imitating our heavenly Father. There are various ways to relate to the love of Christ and understand how it pertains to parenting.

- One of the surest ways to learn about the love of Christ is by hearing it from other people. Quite a number of people have heard from a very tender age that Christ loves them. But for others who have not been familiar with Christianity, have not read the Bible, or have not been churchgoers, it is an astounding experience to hear someone say something about the love of Christ, which was shown by Jesus' dying on the cross of Calvary for the sins of the world. Parents need to say it in the hearing of their children, tell them about the love of God which He has for mankind to the extent that He left heaven and came to the earth to die and ultimately take away the sins of mankind.

- After hearing about God's love, the next thing is believing in the love of Christ. It may not in a day's time, but somehow, along the line comes the belief part. So, when talking to your children about the love of Christ after telling them about it repeatedly, it gets to a point when they actually believe it. The love of Christ and human's receptiveness to it comes in stages as it deepens to the understanding of God's love.

- After the belief comes the assurance that indeed as believers, we have received the love of Christ. Romans 5:5 says,, "And hope maketh not ashamed; because the love of God is shed abroad in our hearts by the Holy Ghost which is given unto us" (KJVS). Let your children come to the realization that they have received the love of God, not for their good works or because they merit it, but because it is God's unconditional love.

- Moving forward, the next process for the believer is being filled with the love of God to the extent where it becomes one's identity in Christ. And, the most beautiful thing to happen to a believer is to be controlled by the love of Christ. His love will show the believer how to love other people without complaint and how to plan activities with God's love. When you are being controlled by God's love, it ensures that other people also get to feel and know the love of Christ. An important reason why we do not fully understand the love of Christ is that most people measure it through little things.

A Standard of Love

We must genuinely love the Lord, who gives us the ability to love our children. Jesus said, "Love the Lord your God with all your heart, with all your soul, and with all your mind" (Matthew 22:37 NKJV).

In John 13:34, Jesus called his followers to a very high standard, "I give you a new command: Love one another. Just as I have loved you, you must also love one another" (HCSB). We are called to love our children and all others, in the way Jesus demonstrated love to us.

Jesus gave us examples of how to love by demonstrating how He loved His disciples, teaching them, and admonishing them. It is commonplace throughout the Bible to see instances of where God loves us and expects us to love other people around us. Still, according to the Scriptures, there is a standard of love that is exemplified in Luke 6:27-36:

> But I say to you that hear: Love your enemies, do good to those who hate you, bless those who curse you, pray for those who abuse you. To him who strikes you on the cheek, offer the other also; and from him who takes away your coat do not withhold even your shirt. Give to every one who begs from you; and of him who takes away your goods do not ask them again. And as you wish that men would do to you, do so to them. "If you love those who love you, what credit is that to you? For even sinners love those, who love them. And if you do good to those who do good to you, what credit is that to you? for even sinners do the same. And if you lend to those from whom you hope to receive, what credit is that to

you? Even sinners lend to sinners to receive as much again. But love your enemies, and do good, and lend, expecting nothing in return; and your reward will be great, and you will be sons of the Most High; for He is kind to the ungrateful and the selfish. Be merciful, even as your Father is merciful" (RSV).

Believers should react to this standard by embracing it and teaching their children about the basics and encouraging them not to deviate from this standard. Before we embrace this standard of love that has been set, we need to understand it and also ensure that our children understand it as well.

Affirmation

The first words recorded in the Gospels spoken by the Father to the Son are words of affirmation: "You are My beloved Son; in you, I am well pleased" (Mark 1:11 NASB). The Greek word for child-rearing, *paideia*, is not limited to parental discipline, but is an all-encompassing word for training and nurture (see 2 Timothy 3:16).

There is no better place to affirm truths about your children than in the Word of God. Those biblical affirmations help strengthen your child. This biblical affirmation will be a source of hope and clarity to your child because the Word of God is adequate. It will help you to see the spiritual growth of your child. Start cleaning the inside. When it comes to parenting, affirmations help prevent negative talk as you speak things into existence. The Word of God changes things around for the better and so daily claims of the Scriptures for your children will change them, renew their minds, and make them better individuals over all.

Tough Love

Tough love is a form of parenting that makes it evident for children to see that although they are loved by their parents, they will not provide an excuse for their inactions and behaviors. It is like a parent saying, "I love you, but I am still going to do what

I have to do, regardless if you like it or not because it is what is good for you."

Tough love, most times is muddled up with authoritarian parenting. When we are talking about strict parents, it is a style of parenting where the primary purpose is for the children to comply with the instruction of the parent instead of teaching any lesson worthy of note. Do not be mistaken; tough love has to do with warmth and empathy because it is from a place of love for the child to learn a lesson that will help in their life's journey.

When it comes to tough-love parenting, it has to do with parents setting limits and clear-cut boundaries for their children that should not be crossed. And for every edge that is crossed, there will be a consequence that will be effected immediately to teach an important life lesson.

One of the reasons why parents may use tough love is to ensure and increase the responsibility of a child. It makes them accountable for their actions and behaviors, and they must own up to their digression. Instead of petting and pampering your child or eradicating the consequences of their actions, tough love will ensure that they experience the consequences of breaking the rules.

Tough love might include setting strict boundaries and letting the consequences of certain actions take full effect to be a memorable lesson to be learned from it, never to be forgotten. Regardless of which one of the above you choose, the reason for it is so that your children will comprehend that you will do everything and anything to aid them in becoming a better person themselves.

So, you are wondering what the principle behind tough love is; it is for you as a parent to care deeply about your child to the point where you are continually setting boundaries and an adequate result of actions if the rules are broken. Tough love, most times, is used for teenagers who are having a hard time being obedient. When these happens, then you need to boldly let the teenager face the consequences of the actions he or she has embarked on, so they will understand why it is not right to be unruly or disorderly. You need to ensure that your child takes responsibility for specific actions taken.

You must let your children know that you genuinely love them, but that will not stop you from disciplining them when the need arises. Parents, you must not be reluctant if there is the need to get professional help coupled with prayers and other necessary things. Let your children be aware of the boundaries and the limits that you have put in place and the need for them to adhere to these boundaries, because they will encounter the consequences involved for the particular action if they do not comply. And it is essential to let the boundaries be consistent. If a child does something today and you say it is totally wrong, then the child does the same thing in a few days and it is not wrong. Inconsistency confuses a child to the point where they do not really know what is right or wrong anymore. Tough-love parenting does not mean there is no room for respect in your parenting, especially teenagers. You need to respect them and the various challenges they face that will transition them into adulthood. Be sure to get the balance between your guidance as a parent and giving them enough freedom to let them live life. Be a leader and be in charge of the situation of your home and your children, manage all conditions, and be on top of it. Controlling the problem doesn't mean holding your child's life in the totality of it. There will be points where you need to relax and let your children make their own choices and watch them experience the consequences of that particular action, either good or bad. Let your children see you as a loving parent that will go the extra mile to make them happy and be there to listen when the situation calls for it.

According to research, children with tough-love parents are twice likely to exhibit good traits and character than those without tough-love parents. And this is because love and consistent discipline are major ways to building the character of children. Empathy is one thing that is discovered in children with strict-love parents. It is also found that the way you parent your children has more influence on them than their status in society. The fact that your children are wealthy or not does not really influence them and their character as much as the parenting style that you use.

Tough-love parenting ensures that parents identify and exercise their power in the family. If your children do not adhere to the laid-down rules and regulations for the family or are rebellious, then it is left to you as parents to create change. You want to effect these changes, and above all, seek God's direction in how to achieve it.

Ensure you have a say in the lives of your children; do not be dictatorial or authoritarian, but be there for them. Live an exemplary lifestyle that will influence your children and allow them to learn from you. To effect change and ensure tough-love parenting, you need to be straightforward and do not give mixed signals to your children. If you are on the path to completely changing your children, it is better you turn back before it is too late. As you cannot completely change your child, all you can do is to effect a change in their character, which might now change their personalities.

Tough-love parenting is sometimes confused with authoritarian parenting, which does not have the same principles of tough-love parenting. Tough love is not an avenue for parents to physically abuse their children or dehumanize them, as this is not what tough love stands for. It is important to identify those things that are not acceptable under the tough love ideologies.

- Tough love does not subscribe to parents embarrassing their children.
- Tough love does not include any form of abuse, whether physical, emotional, financial, etc. Tough love does not support your locking your children out of the house for whatever reason or sending them out of the house permanently. It is not about punishing your children for their transgressions, but ensuring that they change their ways for the better.
- Do not constantly put fear into the hearts of your children to enforce your will on them.

The principle of tough love has been around for a long time and has worked for many families, but for some other families, not so much.

Benefits a Child Can Get From Tough-Love Parenting

There are various ways through which children can benefit from tough-love parenting. And one such advantage is to be independent. If a child is raised with the tough-love parenting and has faced various consequences for the actions taken, it will help reduce the rate at which children utterly rely on their parents for everything. When parents have set boundaries and attach consequences for them, when these boundaries are crossed and the child ultimately faces the consequences, the concept of being responsible for the decisions taken will set in and lead the child to refuse to be subjected to external influences that bring about grave consequences. The child will have an independent mind that will self-direct the decisions and actions since he or she will have to live with the results. Tough-love parenting can encourage a child to think for himself and make decisions based on the advice and admonishment by the parents. The purpose of the tough-love parenting is to teach life lessons, and after these lessons have been learned by the child, it will help shape their thinking and decision-making skills for the better.

Children that were trained with the tough-love parenting find it easy to handle situations and challenges life throws at them. Tough-love parenting shows your child that nothing will be given to them easily without their working for it. This gives the mentality that indeed, it is essential to navigate the workings of the world without expecting aids and reliefs each and every time. Parents should instill the idea of kindness, and kindness coupled with hard work will go a long way in overcoming challenges and trials. Children brought up with tough love early enough learn to accept losses as a variant of life and are not meant to last forever.

Children brought up with tough-love parenting are often humble and devoid of the sense of entitlement. And this is because they have to earn some things, as they are not given to them on a silver platter. And for everything handed to them, they are highly appreciative and do not take them for granted. Humility is greatly valued by a child raised with tough love. They are trained to be confident yet humble and celebrate success moderately. The reality is that tough love is effective only, and if only, it is coupled with love, care, and support.

Do not think for one minute that tough-love parenting is easy. It is not; it might be challenging to implement, since children might decide to be rebellious and challenging too. But if the challenging love strategy is implemented appropriately, then it will help improve the character of your child. So, I am sure the next question on your mind is how exactly can I implement the tough-love policies without my children becoming rebellious?

First, you need to respect your child and respect their decisions also. Rest assured they will learn from their mistakes and be a better version of themselves.

Second, you need to be consistent in your teachings as this will ensure that your children take you seriously and do not take you for granted. Initially, they might be sullen, but with time, they will get the hang of it. As a parent, you need to do what you have to do to make sure that your children turn out well.

Third, you need to be firm enough to make sure no harm comes to your child; the tough-love method might be a little harsh, but if you stay firm, your children will take responsibility for their actions. And the beautiful part is that your children, despite everything, will know that you love and genuinely care for them.

Fourth, let your children know each rule and the consequences attached to it. There must be clarity when it comes to what is expected of them, as they must be aware of the rules. If necessary, let them have a written copy, so they can refer to it from time to time. Be as concise as possible with the rules. You need to parent your children well, to the point where you know their activities and their ups and downs. You need to show your children that you indeed care for them and demonstrate the love you have for them. When you let them know that no matter what happens, you will be there for them, it will encourage them to open up about their challenges and fears.

It should be noted that tough-love parenting is not to be used at all times, as there are situations where it is needed and necessary. One of the reasons to make us of the tough love is if your children are disobedient. If your children are notorious for flouting rules and going scot-free, then you definitely need to implement the tough-love principle as a means to get them back on the right track. If your children make use of their devices after the normal time you have given to them, then it is appropriate to seize it from them until they fully understand the concept of following stipulated rules and regulations.

Also, you can make use of tough-love parenting when you have children who are lazy and not ready to do anything beneficial for themselves. When a child typically ignores or avoids doing chores and other responsibilities allotted to them, establish a measure that will help change the child for the better. And when it is absolutely essential, you might have to withhold some rewards or privileges until they comply with the rules. Sometimes, some children do not remember the vital things they need to do for their own benefit. When this happens, you need to let them not have that benefit for some time. So, the next time, they will easily remember that that is something they need and must take care of.

When it comes to exercising tough-love parenting, you need to be calm and patient so you will not act under the influence of anger and then punish the child instead of disciplining them. Tough-love parenting is birthed from a place of love and not of anger. Tough love makes your children more self-conscious and mature enough to handle situations when necessary.

Most teenagers and youth simply do not understand how their parents loving them includes ensuring they do certain things. This is because tough love is like a parent saying I love you, but I will not hesitate to make you face the consequences of your wrong actions. Actions and values are the tough part of the authoritarian love ideology, since most teenagers tend to think their own idea is the best, and their understanding of life is superb and cannot be faulted. It is not surprising that adolescence comes with some mentality that might not necessarily be correct. They believe their opinion should be final and taken as the absolute one.

For instance, teenagers and young adults think they can adequately take care of themselves without the help and constant checking by their parents. So, mostly there is a tug of war about going out and returning whenever the child deems fit regardless of the curfew time imposed by the parent. This is another instance of needing to bring in tough love as a parent, regardless if your teenage child can take care of himself or not. These children need to be responsible for their actions as they grow into responsible adults. All I am trying to say is that tough love should be implemented as a measure against certain behaviors and actions. It should not be an avenue for you as a parent to unleash brutality on your children. Ensure you make use of the biblical ways of disciplining your children.

When Tough-Love Parenting Is Needed

One reason why parents try to make sure they give their children the best, is so they can grow up to have empathy and kindness for everyone around them. Prior to the age of technology and social media, parenting was not so tricky since parents used various means to train their children. But nowadays, even if parents face their children to correct the wrong they are doing, the parents still have a situation where the children will resist their parents and go ahead with what they want to do regardless of parental opinions and advice. And if you are seen vocally admonishing your children even in the politest manner, you will still have lots of people castigate you and fault your parenting style.

As a result of this, several parents are afraid of the harsh response of other people to their parenting skills, and this has led countless parents to soften their tough-love parenting and just ignore the vices of their children in public, which leads them to excessive anger in private. This does not help with training up your child. So, it is important to state that the level of tough-love parenting varies from family to family and is dependent on the relationship between parents and children. So do not say you want to follow the tough-love pattern of another parent to the letter; do what works for you and parent your children to the best of your ability.

Various Essential Things to Note:

First, identify your values and virtues and pass them on to your children. You cannot do this alone by just talking about it over and over. You can effectively do this by acting it out, letting your lifestyle as a parent highlight your virtues and values. If for you, your most prominent value is giving, then you need to do it often so your children will see it as a way of life and they can easily follow suit without any stress.

Second, do volunteer work, and take your children along. Giving back to society is an excellent thing for a child to learn at a young age. At the end of the day, it makes the world a better place for everyone. Do not think I might be too harsh on my children if I insist they follow me on trips in helping mankind when they clearly do not want to go. Ignore their minimal discomfort as it is for a larger good and the learning of cogent life lessons that will help them in their journey to adulthood and their own parenthood days.

Third, do not hide or be secretive about your core values, let it be known and practiced. Let your children know what the real world is like and how to navigate it properly.

Fourth, do not be quick to join your children in pitying themselves when something did not go their way. Let them know that in this life there are ups and downs and that they cannot expect everything to be perfect. Dissuade them from unnecessary crying as a result of change of plans or an unexpected situation. Teach your children not to take things to heart, but learn from their failures, so that when there is a success they will appreciate it better. And it is also an avenue for them to work on toward achieving success in subsequent times.

Fifth, let your no be no, regardless of the situation or circumstances involved. Do not let the tantrums thrown by your children either in public or private sway your decision, because if it does, it just means that your children already have the idea that the moment they protest and throw a tantrum, you will change your decisions immediately. And this will not speak well as they will begin to take you for granted and even defy your orders at the slightest provocation. The truth is every child is a potential manipulator who can develop various ways to manipulate and compel their parents into doing certain things. They always want their say to be final, and they can go to any lengths to make this happen either by cajoling you or raising up a storm. Let your no be firm and resounding as they might think that whenever they misbehave it will get them whatever they want. And mind you, sometimes they try out the sweet and bubbly behaviors, the hugs, the kisses, the pleading, and even tears just to get their way. Do not allow that to have a substantial effect on you as it is all a ploy to move you to submission.

Sixth, keep in mind you are the parent and your mental capacity cannot be compared to that of your children just yet. There are some certain behaviors you cannot expect from them until they are much older and in the adult stage. For no reason should you punish a child; you should instead discipline him. You cannot expect your children to clean the house like you do or take care of fragile things as you do. Do not think of punishing your children for things like noisemaking or breaking things as a result of anger. Forgive them for their transgressions and discipline them with time out or grounding where applicable and when necessary. Also, explain to them what they have done to warrant the discipline, and if it happens over and over again, you might want to increase the disciplinary period so they willfully understand the extent of their mistakes.

Seventh, do not be overly protective of your child; it will make him dependent on you and he will not be able to do things on his own. Do not let your children see the world as a place where no harm will come to them because you will always be there to protect them. From the time your child is old enough, let them venture out, get a few bruises from playing and then shed a few tears and you will be there to console them and make everything better. This is part of growing up and learning. If you try to keep them indoors and prevent them from really exploring because you do not want them to be hurt, it will affect their self-confidence later on in life. Encourage them and support them and watch them grow into confident adults. It is necessary for you as a parent to let them know that being hurt or having a little discomfort is an integral part of experiencing life.

Eighth, as a parent, do not put undue pressure on your children to be a particular type of person. Just because your friend's son is good at playing the guitar does not mean you have to force your own son to learn to play the guitar. Do not have a particular unrealistic expectation about your child to the point where when he or she does not subscribe to any of your expectations. Let your children just have fun and explore their hobbies; do not choke them with various skills you THINK they might need and curb their own goals. Do not expect your child to be Charles Babbage, and if you are wondering who that is, he is the father of the computer. Let your children grow up and excel at their own pace; do not pressure them and expect them to fulfill a lifelong dream of yours. They have their own life to live, not to compliment or fulfill yours.

Let your children know that no matter what, you will ALWAYS love them unconditionally. When it comes to tough-love parenting, a very integral part is love. No matter what your children do and the decisions they make, you will be there to love forever. Let them be aware of this because it is the absolute truth. You will always be concerned about their wellbeing, even when they have done something wrong. And that the discipline you dish out to them is not because your love for them is faltering, but because you love them too much to let them go astray without any measures to put them in check. Try to help them understand that they can always count on your love for them anytime and any day, because it is as constant as the rising of the sun.

No matter what you do, you cannot absolutely prevent your children from making mistakes and failing in some things. Your child will learn important things from you, but this does not mean they will not fail in some things or make mistakes that might cost them a little. The truth is you as a parent also make mistakes, but rising up and correcting the errors and trying again is the real deal. If they fall a thousand times, they will always rise up again because it is part of human nature to make mistakes, and the best thing is to learn from those mistakes so as not to repeat them. Your child is a unique being and will not be an exact replica of you as they will be different in their own way. As a parent, you will be there to guide them through those moments when they fall and stumble. Let them feel loved and face the consequences of their actions head on; just be there to draw out the lessons for them when necessary.

You cannot deny the fact that you love your children genuinely to the point where you are ready to do anything to make them happy and satisfied. But you should try to be conscious of the fact that your children have a life of their own to live and sooner or later, they will have to go and start their own family away from yours. So, you need to ensure that they are self-sufficient and can face challenges on their own. As a parent, your child is not the absolute essence of your being; you are first you for yourself before you are for your children. Do not be that kind of parent who does not have a life outside of parenting. After the children are grown, you will not know what to do with yourselves, so you will keep pressuring your children to come spend time with you because you are used to always having them around. Try to create "me-time" for yourself to rediscover yourself and build up a life that might not have your children in it very much.

Truthfully, some things are easier said than done because your children can be very persuasive to make you lessen your tough-love parenting. But keep up the idea, the world can be a scary place and you need to fully equip your children to survive the turmoil and make an impact in the world today. Your children might see you as strict and disciplined now, but as time goes by, you will be their hero and go-to person. Be resolute and stand your ground when the situation arises and show love to your children. Create memories with your children: Go on holidays, take vacations, and go for picnics and spread love and light to everyone around you. Raise your children with tough love and enjoy the process all the way.

Unconditional Love

Parents should ensure their children know that you love them unconditionally. When a good foundation of trust and unconditional love is established between a child and its parents, the child is much more apt to view their parents as loving coaches rather than lording adversaries during their time of struggle.

When your child recognizes that your love for them is limitless and that nothing they do or say can ever change that, they will not be as likely to view you as an adversary when the tough times come. Your child needs to be comforted by your love both from praise and from punishment. Be sure to establish their assurance at the youngest possible age. It has been known that parents who wait until the teenage years to try to pull out the "unconditional love" card have face rejection from their teens. Let them hear you say, "I will always love you, no matter what."

It is essential that your child knows, believes, and understands that no matter what decisions they make, and no matter what decisions you make, you are constantly going to fight for what is in their best interest.

Unconditional love is quite imperative, and as parents, you should love your children with your whole heart as it boosts their physical, mental, and even spiritual health.

As parents, you need to love, care, and show affection to your children, regardless of their errors and mistakes—that is called unconditional love. This is a type of love that does not come with any conditions. You need to love your children not because of a particular trait but because of who they are and what they represent. When you are conditional with your love for your child, it gives them the idea that they cannot meet up to the standard that you have created and that they constantly need to always do something to help them earn your love and appreciation. This kind of mentality will lead your child to always be anxious because they are trying to please you enough to get your love and affection. It has been widely known that this kind of ideology will also translate to your child thinking God will only love him/her if he/she does something in return every single time. It has been proven that parents who unconditionally love their children will, at the end of the day, feel accepted and loved by their children. They have built a solid, real, and lasting relationship.

8

ENDURANCE

In the beginning, an infant is entirely dependent on its mother's care. As time advances, children's need for their parents' presence changes, but they continue to need instruction and guidance. Even when children are grown, parents could be present with them through the features they instilled in them. At the same time they were young, they were establishing their ongoing relationship.

There Are Stages of Parenting, and Our Goal Should Be to Maximize Each One
From birth, our children are continually changing. Just like the weather has its seasons, life and parenting are much the same way. Our children naturally go through seasons, phases, or stages of continual growth. And as our children continue to change, they have different needs. As our children change, the parent has other responsibilities. It is essential to reinvent yourself in your children's lives to stay involved in their life.

Being an involved parent takes time, and it is also hard work. Often it means rethinking and rearranging our schedule or our priorities. Staying involved may even mean sacrificing what we want to do for what our child needs to do. As parents, we must be there mentally, as well as physically when we can.

Parenting Generations
Passing godly principles on to the next generations is part of parenting. God needs us to think in terms of ages. We're not only to think of our children, but our children' s children. You, your

son, and your grandson reflect three generations. The principles, teachings, and training will influence the lives of our children and dramatically impact the lives of the next two generations. Deuteronomy 6:2 says, "That thou might fear the Lord thy God, to keep all his statutes and his commandments, which I command thee, thou, and thy son, and thy son's son, all the days of thy life; and that thy days may be prolonged" (KJVS).

Parenting Adults

Adult parenting is a time of sharing wisdom and giving support to your children and grandchildren. We can share memories and stories to pass down by our generations to teach legacy, honor, and standards. This can be a time to show evidence of godliness, faithfulness, and the power of God.

Parenting adults can be a bit challenging from when they were toddlers and teenagers. This is because there are enough resources to surmount those early days, but for parenting adults, there are few resources to go by. There are different stages to adulthood in children as some people believe. Adulthood starts at age 18. The life of a 20-year-old is about college, dating, trying to stick to a career path and explore, while for a "child" in his 30s it is about starting a family, making it big in the career world, and even traveling the world.

It is important to discuss various ways through which you can parent your adult children as it is now time to accept the independence of your child since the age of nurturing and safeguarding is over.

First, parents need to identify the differences in ideology and work on reaching a middle ground. Adult parenting is a new phase and the earlier the better to recognize the uniqueness of your child. You might not agree on everything. Still, it should be common knowledge that you love your child and you need to find a meeting point since there will be more independence for them and you cannot fully enforce anything. You need to lose the critical part of parenting as you need to impact your child now with understanding and insight. The moment your adult child senses criticism in your approach toward them, they shut themselves off and prefer doing things their own way. You need to be very tactical and sensitive in your dealings with your adult child. However, it is challenging to do that since you are used to guiding and helping them every step of the way. But now you need to bond with your child with understanding and effective communication.

Just because your children are adults now does not mean you should not hang out and do fun things together anymore. Go to places where you both frequented when they were teenagers and just hang out and have conversations.

Second, a significant thing that you must be aware of is that now that your children are adults they will most definitely try to build their own relationships and have partners. To you, they are still your babies, but it is time to let other people share their lives with them. So, you need to make room and accommodate their partners as it is essential to let them enjoy their independence. Be cheerful and meet their partners with an open mind and do not be overly critical lest they feel you do not want them to advance in their journey.

Last, do not jeopardize the accessible communication you have built with your children over time. Let your adult children know that they can always talk to you when the need arises and they need help. Be it for guidance, prayers, and even a lesson through the Scriptures. As adults, now, they will do more of the talking to you than actually asking for your opinion on things. Just be there to listen and contribute only when you are specifically requested. Since communication is opened, have family gatherings frequently to keep everyone updated on each other's lives without excessive meddling. Meetings where you can talk about issues, achievements, and future plans.

Reasons for Children's Rebellion

Godly parenting in America today is a very challenging task. And regardless of the various resources in use today as a guide for parenting, we see children rebelling against their parents. This is not strange, as rebellion is an aspect of growing up that is necessary and comes with time. There comes a point in a child's life where he/she rebels against the already laid down rules and regulations. A time will come when a child has to go out into the world on his own and needs to make certain decisions on his own. Various opportunities will show up that will give your child an avenue to become less dependent on you and want to do things by himself. All that is left is for you to do is encourage and give him the support he desires.

But it is not all the time that a parent experiences rebellion in a positive way from their children. Many children rebel in an unhealthy way, and it isn't even fair to blame their rebellion on the parents as they have tried their best. The poor choices of their children are not their fault entirely. It is unfair to think that it is solely the fault of a child for his or her rebellion. Some parents push their children into the world of rebellion. Both children who are brought up in a godly way and those not brought up in a godly manner rebel. Rebellion is not limited to a particular style of parenting. According to Dr. Tim Kimmel in his book, *Why Kids Rebel*, he said there are various reasons why Christian kids rebel, and it is worth looking at to give you as a parent an idea of what you have been doing to push your children into rebellion or, better still valid reasons why children with a Christian parent rebel against their parents and the world at large.

The first of those reasons, according to Dr. Tim, is giving your children rules without adequate explanation regarding the reason for the particular rule. Giving your children rules are imperative without any doubt. When your children are quite young, you need to enforce those rules to keep them in check—simple rules like making sure they say a short prayer before the meal and making sure they are respectful toward elderly people. These rules go a long way in the development of the child. These rules educate children on safety, respect, the difference between what is right and wrong, and also the idea that for every choice, there is a consequence attached to it.

Second, you may think this is simple logic, but an error on the part of the parent is to dish out those rules to the children without proper explanation why the rule exists in the first place. Rules are not ultimate in the sense that they live because they are automatically meant to live; its purpose is to help the parent educate their children on the certain characteristics and values they need to possess. When you explain the rule you have set up for your children, then you provide them with the opportunity to keep those rules. When you do this, you not only help them to be a better person, but you also let them understand that there is a cause and effect factor present. If you did not give any explanation, they will still follow the rules, but they will not understand the essence of the rule in helping build their character. For instance, instead of just collecting all the devices and gadgets when its bedtime and listing out the consequences of not complying with the rule, you can explain why it is needed to reduce the number of hours spent on the Internet. Also, if a child is not well rested, facing the world the next day might be overwhelming. There needs to be time scheduled to read the Scriptures in order to know God more. Let them know the essence of rest and its health benefits in the body. When the understanding of a rule is arrived at by your child and the consequences of not adhering to the rule, then there is the probability that they will fully grasp the essence of the rule and why it must be followed. Let the reason be crystal clear.

Third, the reason why Christian children rebel is because they do not have a second chance when they have made a mistake. Children sometimes unintentionally make huge mistakes, and it is bound to happen sometimes in the journey. Parents need to act when those mistakes are carried out; this is so that the next time it happens or is about to happen, your child knows there is a consequence for the action. The moment parents let a major mistake slide, then the opportunity to make your child learn from the mistake will be lost, but this is not enough reason to make a big deal out of every little mistake. We have already talked about how to discipline your child in love and not mount unnecessary pressure on them to do more. The bottom line is, let your child know that despite their mistake and the discipline that accompanies it, that it all comes from a place of love. Your children need to know that regardless of what they do, you love them and will always love them. Their errors do not change the love that you have toward them, as no one is perfect.

Mistakes and errors are bound to happen to everyone at a given point in time. So as parents, there is a need for you to give room for mistakes to happen without alienating or condemning your children. The fear of rejection will ultimately move them to commit more errors as they will be overly conscious of their attitudes and lifestyle. As a Christian parent you need to have a solid understanding toward mistakes and errors. If you do not, the devil is ever ready to drag them into rebellious acts.

Fourth, as Christian parents it is your duty to let your children know about the existence of God and all His good works. But it is not your duty to force your religion upon them. Let your children attend a Bible believing church with you and let them know about faith being the pillar of Christianity, but do not take the place of the Holy Spirit to convince them. Accepting Jesus as their personal Lord and Savior is a personal decision unto salvation for you and also for your children, especially the teenagers and youths. It is not your role as a parent to ensure the salvation of your children. This is the responsibility of the Holy Spirit. Your role is to make sure you exemplify your own faith in the presence of your children and let them see you as a great example of how they will be if they accept the faith you have been talking about. If you force God and Christianity as a whole on your children, it will translate to them as God being overly strict and possessive, but tell them about it and act it out while praying for them. Enforcing it might bring about a sense of resentment within them which will ultimately lead to rebellion on their part. And with prayers and teaching them the Word of God, watch the miracle happen.

Fifth, parents know that the world today is sinful and is full of violence and fear. The mistake now for parents is to bring up their children in fear. No good parent will want to throw their child into the world full of hate and greed and hence the reason for the fear. But constant fear on the part of the parent is one of the reasons why Christian children rebel against their parents. Agreed, the world is full of evil and the devil is on patrol trying to influence our children, but it should also be noted that God is greater than the deceit of the devil. Bringing up your children in fear and being overprotective, is you admitting that God cannot protect your children. If your level of faith is nonexistent, your children will notice it. When they are finally independent, they will flee from the religion. The fear of the world is not from God and the moment your children notice this, they will rebel and go far away from religion.

Finally, another reason why Christian kids rebel is if they do not see the workings of faith in the life of their parent. As critical thinkers, they tend to look for evidence of "this faith" working for the one who has introduced it to them before they finally subscribe to it. And if they discover it is not working, the moment they are independent they toss it out like trash. The truth about faith is when it is really lived out, it is one of the most exhilarating, and satisfying lives one can live. If it is rightly displayed in front of children and teenagers, the options the world offers will seem empty and unsatisfying.

Love That Never Fails In-Laws

Loving your child's spouse is important for a transition into godly parenting for the next generations. You must overextend your arms of love to help create that healthy needed bridge into that newest phase of parenting in your children's lives. Allow your family to grow in the newest phase of love. Remember, love changes things because God is love. However, the difference is that nothing is impossible with God. The Bible says, What's impossible with man is possible with God (see Luke18:27). Just like you made that sacrifice to allow your own child into your life, you must make that kind of sacrifice to adapt to your child's spouse. The Bible says love can conquer a multitude of faults (see 1 Peter 4:8).

Grand Parenting

This is the time that you get to enjoy parenting without all the daily responsibilities. Parenting ends when we end.

Now that you have parented your children to the point where they build their own families and have their own kids, then indeed you have done your bit and resting is the goal now. But the truth is parenting is for a lifetime and it does not end with your children having their own families now. Now you are in the world of grandparenting and you still have some responsibilities to your grandchildren.

Proverbs 17:6 says, "Grandchildren are the crown of the aged, and the glory of sons is their fathers" (NASB). Your grandchildren are to be taken care of and pampered, but if you think that is your only role as grandparents, then it is grossly inaccurate. You do not just get to sit and "enjoy yourself" because you are done parenting your children. Parenting is a generational thing and the effect of one generation might be transferred to another, from you to your children, and then grandchildren. So, better parenting is done adequately and in a godly manner to ensure a biblical impact on each generation.

Deuteronomy 4:9 says "Only take care, and keep your soul diligently, lest you forget the things that your eyes have seen, and lest they depart from your heart all the days of your life. Make them known to your children and your children's children" (ESV). This part is talking about using your experiences as grandparents to impact godly virtues into your grandchildren. Godly parenting is a lifelong commitment and does not just end after a certain time frame. God still needs you to have a say in the lives of your grandchildren and navigate them in the right path to follow, and they will be able to relate well with you because of the experiences you have gathered.

So, as a grandparent, you are wondering how you can parent your grandchildren without being in the way of your own children's parenting. Sincerely, you had time to parent your own children so it is only normal you give them the opportunity to parent their own children too. You need to pray for your children and grandchildren, constantly pray for them and be specific about your prayer points. You need to pave the way for the ease of your children's parenting by communicating with God about your wants and desires concerning them. Ask for a godly marriage and a Christian home for your children so that training their own children in the way of the Lord will be possible. Ask for wisdom to help them parent your grandchildren properly, and most important request for your help when the going is getting tough.

All you need for them instead of trying to enforce it, is just to put it all into prayers. Ask for growth of their spirit man and the grace to keep growing in our Lord Jesus Christ.

As a grandparent, you need to be available and present in your grandchildren's lives to easily influence them and instill your advice in their spiritual growth. Do not get this wrong; it is not about you hijacking the parenting of your grandchildren from your own children; it is about you just contributing to their success as a whole. Do not be assertive or try to overly criticize the parenting decisions and choices of your children. And it is vital not to overstay your welcome in the situation where you come visiting; as a grandparent you need to try to spend time together with your grandchildren to influence and corroborate the teachings their parents have given to them. If you stay close by your grandchildren, then it makes the visitation easier and if you do not, then it means you will have to plan trips at particular times. And also you can make use of technology to reach out to your grandchildren where it is possible. Video calls, chats and voice calls will go a long way if and when you are not close by. You are still their grandparent regardless of your current location.

What makes you different from their parent is the wealth of knowledge you have amassed over the years, so it is important that you tell them stories of yourself, their parents, and the good old days in general. Even though you want to know everything about them you still need to tell them about exciting events from the past. Talk about how God was faithful to you and your family and how His grace saw you through various trials and challenges, and how you surmount all the typical problems associated with being a youth in your time and as being a parent. Your stories will highlight your own faults in your time and how they should not make the same mistakes.

Be graceful in your grandparenting duties and make it easy for your children to approach you regarding their parenting styles with dealing with their children. There is this idea of parents being reluctant to talk to their own parents because of the difference in their generation or parenting styles. You have done an excellent job raising up your children in the way of the Lord; now it is time to offer your advice to your children while being open-minded. Go the extra miles for the comfort of your children and grandchildren. Try to have fun with your grandchildren and recall various fun memories. Go on long walks, picnics, and vacations. Let your grandchildren see you as someone they can talk to, someone they can confide in, and who is willing to tell them God's view about certain things without mincing words. As grandparents, much more than just having fun with your grandchildren, you need to be able to share the Word of God with them and be their safe place when needed.

CONCLUSION

Raising godly children should not be a one-time thing; it should be a lifestyle, and this is because even after your children, you still have your grandchildren to parent. As a parent, you are fully aware that the world is becoming secular day by day. There is every possibility of the faith of your children being tested because of the secularity in the world. But can you boldly say you are aware of the exact things that can challenge the faith of your children and how to sort them out without stress coupled with the emphasis that always emanates from parenting? Most of the time, the answer to the question is a big NO. A parent might know what the problem in the society is, but proffering a tangible solution to it is a problem. This leads to frustration and fear for the parents as they are scared of the outcome of external influences on the biblical teaching that has been instilled in the child already. Parents are eager to identify those things that can challenge the faith of their children as there are specific conversations to be had with your children so that it becomes easier for your children to navigate through the secularity of life without fatality. It is said that for every problem, there is definitely a solution.

Godly parenting is achievable. Just keep it in mind that first, as a Christian parent, you must have a deep understanding of Christianity itself. I am not talking about just the basics of Christianity without any knowledge of the Word of God, and salvation. In the world of today, the probability of your children experiencing certain things that will challenge their faith is on the increase as we have people who do not believe in God and His wondrous works. Those people are ever ready to state their ideology and the reasoning behind it; they have strong points and premises that support their claim, and they are prepared to enlighten people on it. It is just saddening that many Christian parents are not prepared to educate their children on the truth of Christianity and the exact way to defend their beliefs. There are specific very technical questions that your children have and need answers to. Still, most parents are not equipped adequately to answer those questions.

Even I, remember vividly, as a child, having those profound thinking questions about the existence of God. There were moments I sat in my room and thought deeply about the godly teachings I received and tried to rationalize most of the things I had been told. There were even times, in my teenage years, when I asked myself, *Do I really believe God exists, and if He does, then is He one great magician?* And as time went on, I needed answers to other questions before I could feel confident enough to discuss my faith and what it entails with my friends, when there was a need to do so.

So as parents, you need to answer some questions like what proves that God really exists. And one of the questions that children and even adults alike ask, *If God is truly a loving God, then why is it that He will send people to hell, or allow bad things to happen to good people?* Various questions about the stance of the Bible on persuasive topics in the world today needs to be answered. It is strange that some decades ago, it was easy for Christian parents to avoid questions bothering the mind of their children that have to do with their faith, and that should be addressed immediately because the society was nominal then. But now it is important that you take responsibility for these questions and give befitting answers. Parents need to be equipped when it comes to the knowledge of the Bible. Be intentional about addressing the problems that your children have concerning their faith to help them understand the Word of God more than ever before.

To achieve godly parenting as a Christian parent, you need to do more than understand Christianity and its doctrines. You need to make space for spiritual exercise in your home. When you have a clear understanding of Christianity, the next thing is for you to help your children understand everything. How can you do this if you do not make time and room for those discussions and sessions?

The kind of conversations that you need to have with your children that are based on their faith is definitely not going to happen except you make time and create space to talk about these spiritual matters. Remember to carve out time specifically for you as a family to sit down and discuss your spiritual growth and communication with God. Have a scheduled time for this as you plan a time for other things. It does not have to be hours upon hours; you can begin with 30 minutes and then increase the time you spent talking about those things as everyone gets comfortable with it.

Study the Word of God with your children, as this is quite important for them. They need to fully understand what is written in the Bible to make it easy for them to face critics and atheists in case they are being influenced negatively. The way you treat the Word of God is how your children will treat it too; if they only see you open the Bible on a Sunday, then what that translates to them is that it is not as important as you make it seem and that there is no need to pay particular attention to what it says. Much more than letting your children see you read the Bible, there is a place of a joint study with your children. Let them read out of the passage for the day and share their opinion about it before you share yours with them. Let it be like a conversation, nothing too official that it will defeat the purpose of the study. Let your children be calm and relaxed and discuss God in His entirety with them and what they stand to gain when they follow the Father's lead. The moment you do not show your children the value of the Word of God, they will start ignoring and not caring about what the Bible says.

Godly parenting cannot thrive under an authoritarian parenting style; you need to encourage your children and allow them to ask questions and voice their opinion on things. And if they are out of line, you guide them in love. Your children frequently hear about things that are contradictory to their faith and so their need to ask questions will be on the rise. And if you are not the approachable kind of parent, it might be difficult for your children to walk up to you and ask the questions on their mind. This could be because they are unsure of the kind of reaction they will expect from you or if you will blow it out of proportion and defy the essence of the question in the first place. Let your children know that they can ask their questions whenever they have them as you are there to thoroughly answer their questions to the best of your ability. Get your children to ask questions and sometimes you can ask them to ask you any item of their choice and see how well it will help in your parenting journey.

The moment you make it easy for your children to ask you questions, you will discover that lots of memorable conversations will spring from it between you and your children. There are pertinent questions that your children might not even think to ask or bring up, so it's essential for you to ask your children those questions. Do not wait until your child has to go through a particular challenge before you think it is right to bring up issues about it. Children will meet people who will say things that will get them thinking later on in life; it is essential that you give them teachings about it in advance and prepare them for what it is to come. Godly parenting is intentional and challenging, but you have God to enable you with the know-how and answers.

I hope this book has been a blessing to you and will act as a guide in your parenting journey, as you commit to God, His principles, give godly teaching, and love.